Systemic Leadership

Systemic Leadership

Jan Jacob Stam and Barbara Hoogenboom

Translation by: Barbara Piper

Originally published under title: Tegen de stroom mee – Systemisch leiderschap

© 2018, Systemic Books Publishing

ISBN 978-9492331472 (NUR 801)

All rights reserved. For copying please contact:
contact@systemicbooks.com

Contents

Introduction 1

1 **Summary and Reader's guide** 5

2 **What is 'systemic' all about?** 11
   2.1 It is about systems 12
   2.2 Systems have (repeating) patterns 15
   2.3 Change starts with acknowledging the world as it is 17
       2.3.1 You become what you try to avoid 17
       2.3.2 Acknowledging reality: a healing movement 18
   2.4 Problems are solutions 21
   2.5 Perceiving without judgment, in the present 23
       2.5.1 Systemic perception 26
       2.5.2 Not-Knowing 30
   2.6 Three Survival Mechanisms 32
       2.6.1 Survival of the individual (unit-conscience) 35
       2.6.2 Survival of the system as a whole (system conscience) 37
       2.6.3 Surviving the large flow of development (Evolutionary Force) 39
   2.7 The workings in survival mechanisms 42
       2.7.1 In the Unit conscience 43
       2.7.2 Within the System-Conscience 56
       2.7.3 Within the Evolutionary Force 58

3 **Nurturing your systemic leadership** 67
   3.1 Two basic needs of every system: autonomy and well-being 68
   3.2 Systemic Leadership in three survival mechanisms 72
       3.2.1 The unit conscience 72
       3.2.2 The System Conscience 73
       3.2.3 The evolutionary force 77

3.3	Completeness, including truly everything (Belonging)	78
	3.3.1 The origin	79
	3.3.2 History	82
	3.3.3 Systemic ownership	83
	3.3.4 Can you fúlly welcome your new colleagues?	85
	3.3.5 Place and function	85
	3.3.6 Loyalties, conflicts of loyalty and Objections	91
	3.3.7 Terrible things	92
	3.3.8 No and Yes	92
3.4	Everything has a place (order)	93
	3.4.1 Order in Leading principles	94
	3.4.2 Order in functions	98
	3.4.3 Contribution to the whole	103
	3.4.4 Seniority	104
3.5	Honesty in taking and giving (exchange)	106
	3.5.1 Between the mutual parts	106
	3.5.2 Exchange between the organisation and the outside world	108
	3.5.3 Funding	108
	3.5.4 Money	110
	3.5.5 Influence and Power	111

4 Patterns — 113

4.1	Patterns, Habits and Procedures	114
4.2	How patterns form	114
4.3	The function of patterns	116
4.4	Patterns attract patterns	117
4.5	Getting rid of patterns	119
	4.5.1 Becoming aware of the pattern	119
	4.5.2 Untangling	120
	4.5.3 Growing beyond	122
	4.5.4 Disrupting	123
4.6	Common Patterns	124
	4.6.1 Ending up at your managers level	125
	4.6.2 Ending up above you managers level	132
	4.6.3 Taking on someone else's tasks	139
	4.6.4 Carry out a task because of an unconscious promise	143
	4.6.5 Seeing something different than is there	146
	4.6.6 Connected to what is no longer here	151
	4.6.7 Extremes collide	157

		4.6.8	It will go south if we do it and it will go south if we don't	165
		4.6.9	Success prevented!	170

5 Organisational topics from a Systemic Perspective — 173
- 5.1 Innovation — 174
- 5.2 Person and function — 174
- 5.3 Presence — 176
- 5.4 Which system? — 177
- 5.5 Freeing the function — 177
- 5.6 The face of competition — 179
- 5.7 Control — 179
- 5.8 Feedback or Feedforward — 181
- 5.9 Love and dedication: curse or blessing — 183
- 5.10 Naughtiness as a source — 184
- 5.11 New function — 185
- 5.12 Filling the post — 187
- 5.13 Systemic Competence Management — 188
- 5.14 Cynicism — 188
- 5.15 Skepticism — 189
- 5.16 Judgments — 189
- 5.17 Three kinds of 'we' — 190

6 Transformation — 193
- 6.1 Elements of Transformation — 195
- 6.2 The Unit Conscience — 197
  - 6.2.1 The principle of Belonging, during transformation — 198
  - 6.2.2 The principle of Exchange, during transformation — 201
  - 6.2.3 The principle of Order, during transformation — 202
- 6.3 The System-conscience — 202
- 6.4 The Evolutionary Force — 204
- 6.5 Ba and Ya — 206
- 6.6 Holding Liminal Space — 211
- 6.7 Facing future trauma — 213
- 6.8 Transformative Phase — 214
  - 6.8.1 First order interventions — 214
  - 6.8.2 Second order interventions — 214
  - 6.8.3 Third order interventions — 217

More from these authors — 221

Sources and Literature	222
Jan Jacob Stam	224
Barbara Hoogenboom	225
Guest writers	227
Bert Hellinger Institute the Netherlands	229
About Barbara Piper	230
About Systemic Books	231
Index	231

Introduction

To get straight to the point; systems lead. They lead the whole and they lead the individual. And can you lead something that leads itself? Yes and no. It's about leading and following, about knowing and acknowledging, about going with the flow ánd going against the flow.

Sometimes, it's necessary to swim against the current of life for a while, to find a meaningful source there and continue to float on the force of the organisational system.

This book doesn't aim to tell you how to go about it, systemic leadership. Once you understand and can feel your way through the basic principles that apply to systems, you will undoubtedly find ways to compose your own systemic leadership. The fact that you are in a function or position that requires your leadership, means that you possess the responsibility and power to make something of it.

What we can tell you, is what a system needs of leadership. We will do this by explaining the underlying principles and giving examples of them. Your systemic intelligence and creativity will do the rest. What this book is truly not about, is about you as a leader. Of course, because you are part of an organisation, you are part of a system and it is useful to be aware of your role. Because you are part of the organisation, you are part of the system. You also can't escape the fact that the patterns of all those systems that have made you who you are today, work through you and will affect your team and the organisation.

The message of this book, isn't that you have to work hard at yourself, at your personal leadership skills. We assume that this is something you do often and automatically. That is what your position demands of you. What we do want to show you, is how organisations can blossom and flow, from a systemic perspective. And what leadership is needed to that avail.

The systemic perspective and systemic leadership aims to add to all those other, well known, ways to look at an organisation: legal, financial, business, psychological, organisational science, change management etc…

And: we deliberately speak of leadership. Not the leader him or herself. We explain what a system needs from leadership and what it can win from systemic awareness. With this, we are not saying whó should take up the leadership role or whére the systemic awareness could expand. Systemic leadership could lie with the leader of the organisation or with the team leader. But it could just as well be allocated to different places or people in the organisation. We can well imagine that an entire team ensures systemic leadership. In short, we disconnect what a system needs of leadership, from the leader himself.

Today, we constantly see a demand for new ways or organising and leading. Networking, self-directing, flat organisational structures and so on. Often, 'traditional organisations' are put opposite those. Often, the search for new forms of organisation is born out of a reaction against existing forms of organising. And that in itself has a systemic risk. The more you oppose 'traditional' organisations, the higher the chance that you will become like them. The other thing that happens when you 'oppose', is that the world is split into good and bad. We are caught in a polarity.

The good thing about wondering what a system needs in terms of leadership, is that it applies to any kind of system and to any kind of organisation. For large, hierarchically organised companies as well as for start-ups, fast growing companies and everything in between. Looking Systemically to what is asked of us in terms of leadership eliminates the division between old and new, large and small, hierarchical and flat, sexy and dull, flexible and rigid etcetcetc. Moreover, we might possibly move beyond these kinds of divisions.

INTRODUCTION

On our way to new adventures! It's up to you, to all of you and to all of us to give this shape. Enjoy this book!

Jan Jacob Stam and Barbara Hoogenboom

Summary and Reader's guide

1

Summary

A team, collaboration, start-up, department or organisational system needs the following of leadership:

- That all members have a place and feel that they belong sufficiently so that they are able to do their work well.
- That it is clear-cut what the team as a whole, stands for and what their leading principles are.
- That every person's talent can prosper.
- That the whole of what the team produces can achieve something in the outside world, can reach a destination.
- That rebels are heard because they have important information about the system as a whole.
- That there is an order that provides for enough security, safety, clarity and guidance.
- That there is a good balance between yes and no.
- That it's clear what we do and what we don't.
- That there is enough autonomy for the team as a whole, without being separated from the rest of the organisation or the outside world.
- That there is enough connection, flow, inspiration and energy fuel inside the team.
- That there is discipline and willingness to investigate how problems are a systemic response first, before starting to look for solutions or treating the symptoms.
- That patterns rise to the surface from below which causes them to work fór the system instead of against it. Especially with change and development.
- That the origins and history of the organisation are acknowledged, including the trauma's and events (instead of trying to forget the unsettling events).

- That a distinction is made between the future and the future as it approaches us. And is able to switch between the two adequately.
- That deep commitment is given to the transformational processes which ask enormous elasticity from leadership, with not knowing how the organisation will end up being.

Reader's Guide

We will do something here that we prefer not to do, we will be taking a detour. We would have preferred to tell you immediately in the first chapter what a system demands of leadership. But because organisational systems are such specific things, with sort of a will of their own, we can't escape building a robust stage about what systems are and how they behave in chapter 2 first.

In chapter 3, we can then mount the stage from the leaderships' perspective. What do systems require of leadership and how can you respond to that? A chapter to give you pause for thought as well as energy and ideas.

Chapter 4 zooms into the phenomenon of patterns in organisations. How do they arise, how you can recognise them and what you can do about or with them? It teaches you to better understand the 'below-the-surface-driving-forces' of your colleagues, your organisation and yourself.

Chapter 5 examines a few widespread organisational themes from a systemic perspective. To tickle systemic awareness a little but also to invite you to look at different situations, that you probably deal with at work on a regular basis, from a systemic perspective. It's possible that, after reading this section, you will think of things that are familiar to you in a different way altogether. 'Fuss' gets a whole new perspective.

Chapter 6 is, as far as we are concerned, cutting edge material: transformation. As we speak, the world is full of noise around transformation. And yet there are so few anchors. And you are not getting anchors here either, but we will drench you with what transformation asks of leadership from a systemic perspective.

There where you read JJS and BH, it's about examples or comments of the authors Jan Jacob Stam (JJS) and Barbara Hoogenboom (BH). Other initials refer to a few guest authors, who have added some real-life examples. You can read more about them at the back of the book, where we mention our sources.

Constellations

Much of the knowledge you read in this book, was acquired over the course of eighteen years through the, now reasonably well-known, method of 'constellations'. This book is not about constellations. But there are, however, examples in the book where we draw on our experiences in constellations that we set up with clients. For that reason, we want to give you some context.

A constellation is a spatial representation of an organisational (or other) system. The parts that are relevant to the issue at hand, are set up: e.g. the board, the owner, the team, clients, the goal, the product. These elements are set up in the space éither with objects (cups, glasses, post-its, wooden objects) ór with people, in relation to each other according to an inner image. These people representing elements, we call representatives. They can also set-up themselves. Strangely enough, a constellation gives a very direct image once you are in it: a sensation of the relations and patterns above and below the surface in the organisation. It brings conscious as well as unconscious information from the system to light.

In consultation with the person asking the question, the person leading the constellation can test and intervene to find out what the systemic 'cause' could be of the present situation and what the system needs. A director recently turned to her team after the first constellation and said: *"This afternoon was worth more than six hundred hours of meetings together"*. The impact of a constellation is often profound and long-lasting.

How a constellation works exactly, is still something we don't exactly know. That it works has been scientifically proven sufficiently.

Guiding a constellation is a specific craft and requires a high degree of professionality. In the future, we don't see thousands of managers accompanying constellations during their team meetings. We do see thousands of managers, owners and employees apply systemic knowledge, as described in this book, in their daily work.

What is 'systemic' all about?

2

Systemic is a word that we introduced years ago and today is widely used. What we mean by it, can best be explained using the following principles:

1. It is about systems;
2. Systems have (repeating) patterns;
3. Change starts with acknowledging the world as it is;
4. Problems are solutions;
5. Perceiving without judgment, in the present;
6. There are three survival mechanisms that operate in family, organisational and societal systems.

2.1 It is about systems

What is a system? This sounds so technical and abstract. Hardly human. But that is exactly what it is! Especially! A family unit constitutes a system. A school class constitutes a system. A team constitutes a system. An organisation constitutes a system. A region, country or society constitutes a system.

A system means that, beyond the boundaries of that system, things look different than they do on the inside. Things are different within the family unit of my neighbour than in ours. This is something you know instantly when shoes need to come off as you enter your neighbours' home. Or the type of jokes that you can't make any more in your new team. It takes a little time to figure out the written and unwritten rules. You can sense that the rules aren't your colleagues' rules or the rules of your team manager, no, they are the rules of the entire department, the system that together forms the department.

Barbara Hoogenboom

Our eldest son just started playing baseball. At the sports complex, the baseball field is directly adjacent to the football field. The first parent I met at the side of the field, immediately said: "Oh, you should

CHAPTER 2. WHAT IS 'SYSTEMIC' ALL ABOUT?

be só grateful that your son decided to play baseball instead of football! It's a world of difference what you hear and see there compared to what you see and hear here!"

What you need to know about a system are two things:

1. The system as a whole has different characteristics than the sum of parts
2. A system is always part of a larger system

The system as a whole has different characteristics than the sum of parts

A so-called ghost-traffic jam on a motorway moves exactly in the opposite direction than the car's do, the individual parts. A traffic jam starts because it is busy on the motorway, someone breaks slightly too hard, the driver behind him has to break even harder because of the response time and a few cars down, traffic slowly comes to a halt and stops. Viewing this from the air (I was lucky to experience this once when circling above Schiphol airport) you can see that when the individual cars move in one direction, the entire caterpillar of the traffic jam moves exactly in the opposite direction. Indeed, at the front the traffic jam is dissolving and at the rear end the traffic jam is growing. The funny thing is that drivers who are actually in the traffic jam, often don't know how big the entire system is and that the system is moving in a different direction than they are. It works this way in families, organizations and societies too: the whole has different characteristics than the sum of parts.

The whole moves exactly in the opposite direction than the parts do.

Each of the team leaders in a tax department of a municipality, function perfectly well, but the whole, called the department management team, was stuck.

The whole behaves differently than the sum of parts. The question that immediately arises: should we intervene between the parts, the team leaders or do we intervene in the whole, called the Management team?

What next? Do we intervene on the parts or in the whole?

Think about it: if you are in a meeting, are you more inclined to intervene between the people involved or in the whole?

A system is always part of a larger system. Your function is part of a team. Your team is part of a department. The department is part of a business unit, and so on. It's vital to be aware of the fact that patterns in the larger systems often spill over to sub systems. This is often apparent in conflict. Most conflicts that we see in teams, are reflections of unsolved conflicts in the wider system around them. Like in a hologram.

Jan Jacob Stam

Recently, a woman, who works in a team that deals with domestic violence and child abuse, called me. "Our team works together wonderfully, we do good work. But somehow, we don't take good care

CHAPTER 2. WHAT IS 'SYSTEMIC' ALL ABOUT?

of ourselves. There are tensions within the team. Would you be willing to come and work with us?" *My response, after I let the situation lie for a while, was:* "Have you ever stopped to think that it could be possible that the patterns of the families you work with are spilling over to your team and has grabbed hold of you?" *For a second, it's quiet on the other side of the line:* "Oh, would you please come see us just to tell us this? It's spot on!"

It's the fastest contribution to systemic consciousness that I have ever made!

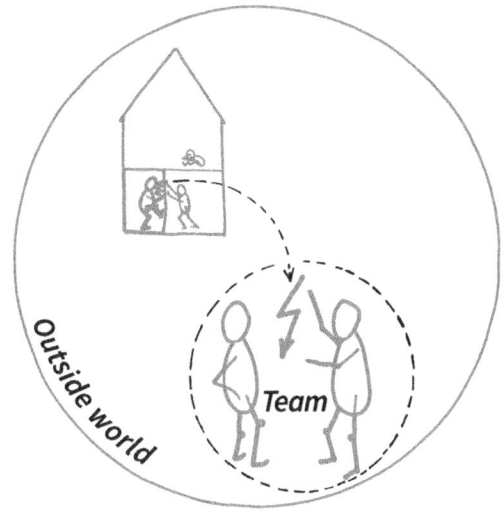

Patterns form the outside world, that you deal with in your work, can spill over to the team. This usually happens unconsciously.

2.2 Systems have (repeating) patterns

A pattern is an unconscious, repetitive set of actions or relations to each other that has to do with people's positions in a system.

The consultancy where I used to be partner, had a pattern that people felt better than management. Openly, we would always emphasize that we were looking to work together with the management of

Jan Jacob Stam

our clients, but in the undercurrent, we always felt better than management. So, with every new client, the recurring pattern would be that we took up position abóve the client and not néxt to the client or únder the client. That was the pattern in relation to our clients. And yes, our expertise was to know what was good for the organisation, and then suddenly, you find yourself above it.

Repetitive patterns are the phenomenon that a pattern repeats itself in more than one sub-system.

Jan Jacob Stam

Within our consultancy, there was always the hidden tendency to feel better than your colleague, even if you there was openness about working and learning together.

This pattern was found amongst the peers of the consultancy that entered at the same time, but also amongst the seniors that wanted to become partner. And within the partnership.

It won't surprise you that, when recruiting new colleagues, there was an unconscious selection of people that were familiar with this pattern of 'putting yourself above another or above something'.

Systemic work is often about making unconscious patterns visible. It is about being conscious where patterns are functional and where they can be damaging. And obviously, about what you can then do with those patterns.

Patterns aren't always enjoyable, because they can be confronting and tough. They also bring predictability and continuity. If you think your organisation could benefit from a deeper knowledge of systems, chapter 4 awaits you.

CHAPTER 2. WHAT IS 'SYSTEMIC' ALL ABOUT?

2.3 Change starts with acknowledging the world as it is

There are hundreds of theories on change. For many of these theories, the starting point is that something needs to change. That the world, an organisation, a person can't be accepted as it is today.

Using the systemic perspective, the starting point for change is: acknowledging the world as it is. This is a fundamental difference. Not better or worse than the other change-approaches, but different. Because 'acknowledging the world as it is', has far reaching consequences for the attitude of the leader and of leadership.

There are a few simple reasons why it is important to acknowledge the world as it is:

- You become what you try to avoid
- Acknowledgment is one of the most healing movement in systems

2.3.1 You become what you try to avoid

What you fight, will detour and return back into the system. This is how systems work. What you don't accept as part of the world, comes back into your school, team, organisation like a boomerang. The more you don't want to become like your mother, the greater the chance you will become like her. We all know that systemic principle.

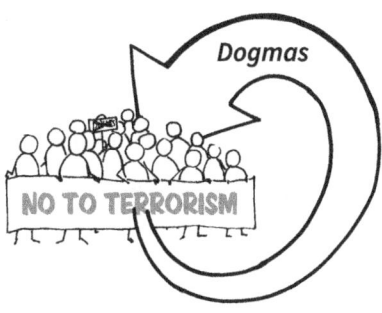

What you want to get rid of, easily comes back in through the back door.

We have had the opportunity to work for peace-organisations a few times where the complaint was: it's war in the boardroom. Think about what your organisation is trying to fight. What is not allowed to be?

Jan Jacob Stam

A man is founding an addiction rehabilitation centre. He is driven. And yet, it's not going so well. I wonder if his drive stems from his own attempts to accomplish something or because he is trying to keep something at bay. It feels like the latter. So, I ask him: "Is addiction allowed to be?" His answer, soft: "No…" Immediately, he feels where the problem lies. We don't need any further talking. Immediately, it is as if you can see him drop into himself and go through a layer and he suddenly finds solid ground beneath him. Addiction is part of this world.

2.3.2 Acknowledging the, sometimes raw, reality is the most healing movement in systems

Acknowledging is admitting to yourself and others that reality is the way it is.

Acknowledging that the accident at work is now forever part of the history of the organisation. Stop wanting that it had never happened. Stop not wanting to see it because it is painful. In chapter 4 you will read that, not-acknowledging, hiding away the event or situation because it is too painful, is what causes a pattern, to remind the system of the events.

Under all of this is the deep realisation: it is reality that heals, not our dreams, wishes and expectations. Contact with reality brings us back to earth and gives us ground. Literally, ground your very existence.

Barbara Hoogenboom

The question put forward for the constellation, was the director of an international organisation that had been owned by a parent company for years. When he said: "I wish the parent company would

CHAPTER 2. WHAT IS 'SYSTEMIC' ALL ABOUT? 19

take us seriously", what was reality? That they dídn't in fact take them seriously! And what would the sentence that leads to change be? "Maybe, we should live with the fact that they will never take us seriously." Hard and true. By acknowledging this, it may be possible that something changes reality.

Who knows, new possibilities and initiatives will arise after the acknowledgement. Especially, by fully taking the role of young rascal!

All wishes, be it from yourself, employees, colleagues, shareholders, start with realising: what you wish for is not here nów. Thát is reality. That is what we need to take. That reality is what we need to look in the eye instead of fleeing it.

Painfully seeing that your boss or your father isn't available for you, gives you more vitality, than being under the illusion that it will be different someday.

Mind you: acknowledging something doesn't mean that you are pleased about it! Of course not, it's painful and you would rather that it wasn't true. And still, if it is 'true', then in all the discomfort, with all the emotions that come with that, it is better to acknowledge: I stop with wanting to fight this. You surrender to it, that it is the way it is. Full stop.

Example	*A department coordinator wants his manager to be more available to him. He wants to receive more compliments and more work-related conversations that matter. There is probably a valid personal or professional reason that the manager is unavailable. Wanting to change a manager is an illusion that consumes energy and where someone can 'remain stuck' for the rest of their functioning in the organisation.*
	The changing movement that shows is: "I have to live with it, that my manager will never truly see me". Thát is the moment where change becomes possible for the coordinator. The change could be that the coordinator decides to leave ór decides to take responsibility for what is possible and/or find different ways to fulfil the need to have work-related conversations that matter.

Look at all the goals you have in your organisation. Can you face them, per goal:

- That your goal isn't there now. And can you do it without blaming yourself or without remorse?
- What the current situation in your organisation is? And acknowledge that? And even love it, the beauty and the charm of imperfection?

> *Who doesn't have hope, has everything*
>
> **Bert Hellinger**

For systemic leadership, the question remains: Which reality do we need to face to take the next step? Which reality is too painful to see? Systemic leadership knows: as long as reality hásn't been expressed, it works like a demon or a dragon. It keeps coming and drawing attention and energy to itself. As soon as reality is expressed, and acknowledged by the team, a new truth emerges, a new movement. Often with an enormous sigh of relief.

CHAPTER 2. WHAT IS 'SYSTEMIC' ALL ABOUT?

Working with entrepreneurs in Venezuela was often emotional. In their entrepreneurship, most of them tried to regain the old, prosperous and free Venezuela. Their home, their dream! But they also got stuck in the new rules of the game in Venezuela. Government 'taking' their companies from them; fraud; treachery. Their dream increasingly becomes a burden. The moment they realised that their old Venezuela wouldn't ever return, enormous amount of energy was released. Contributions to a possible new Venezuela, without knowing what that would look like, gave new momentum and new energy!

Example

While writing this book, I spoke to a few people who are involved with the reconstruction of the earthquake area in Groningen, The Netherlands. At the moment, a major repair project and reconstruction program is being executed. Damaged houses are being repaired and buildings solidified to deal with future earthquakes. But what a lot of people are saying is: "What I really need is acknowledgement for how these earthquakes affect me as a person." "Acknowledgement for the emotional damage that was done." "Acknowledgement for the fact that we all made errors in judgment." "And it is this acknowledgement that they are not getting."

Jan Jacob Stam

2.4 Problems are solutions

> *Problems want to be understood, not solved.*
>
> **Anton de Kroon**

Resistance, cynicism, skepticism, repeated fraud. All unpleasant phenomena in your organisation. Many of these have a systemic edge. And if you look at it systemically, a new perspective may suddenly arise.

A phenomenon that is experienced as a problem in the organisation, is often 'merely' a reaction of the system to what is happening or about to happen. The more you understand how problems are 'solutions' of the system, the more, new perspectives you will find to deal with it.

Let's look at a common 'problem' like resistance:

Resistance is often a, conscious or unconscious, loyalty to that which has been lost or is at risk of being lost. If innovation means we need to say goodbye to an old accounting system that, although it wasn't perfect, was familiar, then resistance is an attempt to prevent something that was part of the organisation, to be excluded. The recipe? The more you recognise and acknowledge that some employees, however much they grumbled about the old accounting system, are unconsciously more connected to it than they thought, the less they will try to 'protect' the accounting system.

The starting point: 'problems are solutions' means you can't find solutions to problems in a direct way. You find solutions in a roundabout way. By first finding out how the problem is a reaction of the system. The price of the detour, is that first you need distance yourself from the problem a bit, or even great deal. Systemic leadership asks of you to endure, or even embrace the problem. Those who want instant solutions, will find this aspect of systemic leadership a hard nut to crack

An illustration. A problem could be that an employee helps him or herself to properties, money, time, or otherwise, that he or she isn't entitled to. Could it be that, unconsciously, a balance needs to be restore in the exchange? A way around to get from problem to solution could be, to verify where, in the history of the organisation there was an imbalance. Can you recall a period of time where people were underpaid? Does the mere existence of the organisation ask too much of the social environment, of nature? Has, somewhere in time, the fact that the organisation exists, required unreasonable sacrifices?

CHAPTER 2. WHAT IS 'SYSTEMIC' ALL ABOUT?   23

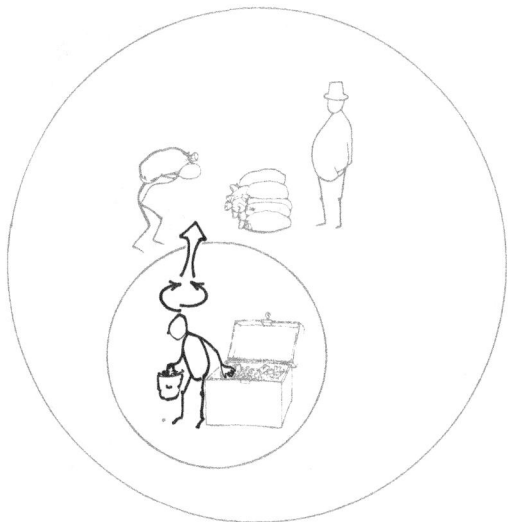

Fraud or corruption of today is an unconscious attempt to compensate for exploitation in the past.

2.5 Perceiving without judgment, in the present

The systemic approach is and is called phenomenological. Phenomenology is about wanting to learn to understand a phenomenon, in the way it presents itself to you. It doesn't focus on specific things and their coherence, but on the essence of the whole, and form an intuitive and open attitude. In other words, the concept 'phenomenological' is best explained by setting it on the other side of the concept analytical.

When you research something analytically, you look in a focused way. You look at details. You try to understand how the details relate to one another. To this end, you measure meticulously. You look at cause and effect relationships. And then you can predict. It is the most common scientific approach. Without this analytical approach, we wouldn't be driving cars, piping natural gas and our medical science wouldn't have made the staggering progression it has.

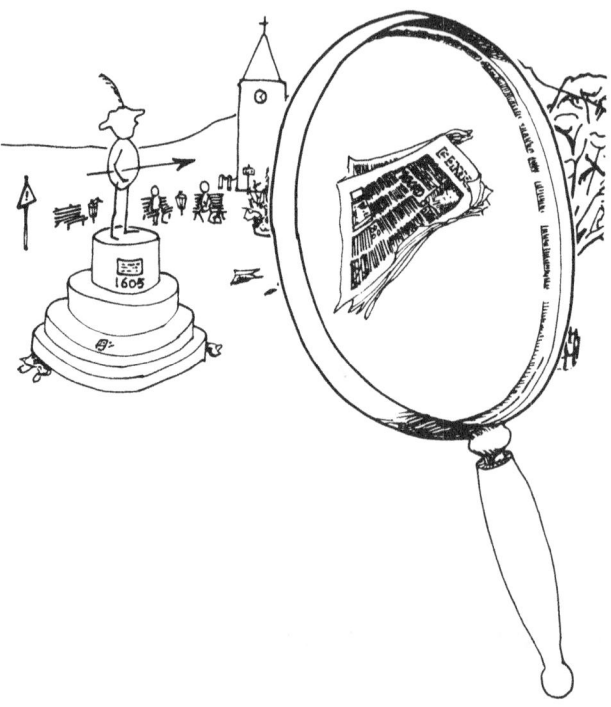

Analytical perception is mainly about zooming in. Which details will help us see the cause and effect connections?

In the phenomenological approach, you take reality, as is presents itself to you, to be true. In this moment. You don't look for reality, but you expose yourself to how reality presents itself to you. You don't read the name tag and growth chart of that red rose, but you open yourself up to what the rose is telling you about life and its beauty.

CHAPTER 2. WHAT IS 'SYSTEMIC' ALL ABOUT?

You don't look, you see
You don't listen, but hear
You are aware
You observe
And you wonder:
What is the whole trying to tell me?
What makes that things will be as they will be?
What can I feel right beneath the surface,
but can't touch, see or name?

Systemic perception is all about zooming out with the question: What is this village trying to tell us? Which patterns and pattern-repeats are thrusting themselves on us? And especially, what is not happening and not visible?

I share this hobby with a group of friends: we venture out to an unknown area, for instance Ameland (an Island just off the Dutch coast) and we try to find out what is going on, systemically, with the place, and what the underlying patterns are.

When, late at night, I arrive on the island, there is really only one thing on my mind: I want to get up as early as possible and bike through the villages as soon as I can. I allow the villages to sink in. I see the way the Islanders walk, how they open their shops. I talk to a few people. Out of genuine interest. Without intent, no different than asking: "what is approaching me, what is this Island trying to tell me?".

Jan Jacob Stam

I see Ameland as a crime scene. You can only arrive at a crime scene for the first time ónce. Hence the morning rush. You can only expose yourself ónce to what the crime scene wants to tell. In the past, something must have happened to make things the way they are today. Often, you can't see that immediately. It can sometimes take days, long after the outing with my friends had taken place, before a penny drops and an insight, often in an unguarded moment, will come to me.

After that first time, I can always return for more, often for more trace evidence. But that first time, that first investigation is always in service of the phenomenological view.

2.5.1 Systemic perception

Systemic perception is a different, and easier, term for phenomenological perception. It is an important element of systemic awareness and of systemic leadership. You observe a situation with soft eyes and with an open heart and mind. In a sense, you turn on different ways of perceiving.

Looking

With systemic perception, you look at your team, as if you see them for the very first time. That is hard. And it gets harder the longer you have been their leader and the longer you have been in the team. You need to consciously step out as often as you can. Sometimes literally.

Or you view them through your eyelashes. You don't look at details but to the whole, the taste, atmosphere, what's in the air? Maybe it is more about 'seeing' than 'looking'.

Jan Jacob Stam

As the manager of a telecommunication company, I sometimes observed perceived systemically by driving to work in the morning, suck up whatever it is I found there, and then leave and spend the rest of the morning in a café in town. With excellent coffee, mind you, otherwise it doesn't work. And then, from a distance, I let what I found

CHAPTER 2. WHAT IS 'SYSTEMIC' ALL ABOUT?

> *sink in. And of course, I would also see myself hanging around there as the companies' manager.*

Wondering about the whole

What is approaching me? What do I perceive? To what extent do I see óne team, or do I see sub-teams? Will it work, what we are here to do in the larger organisation? What am I missing? What is it trying to tell me? What wants to be seen? What did we forget?

Wondering in the conversation

Which words that you hear are charged?
What is not being said?
What stands out, is illogical or unusual?
Which images or associations come up for you while you look and hear? With systemic perception, you don't just look at what someone is sending, but mainly at what is coming through someone. Every person is connected to many systems. If you look and listen to someone, observe from which system someone is speaking.

> *The team leader of a finance department is not only his own person, but also the function of team leader, as well as the previous team leader that left in a bad way, as well as the colleagues in the finance team, as well as their clients, as well as the financial director that feels they should downsize and so on!*

Example

What bodily reactions do you see in them? What are the hands doing? Does the colour of their cheeks change? Do you see tension change in the eyes or jaws? Or is someone touching a jewel that is of importance to him?

Sometimes you notice someone's voice change. He speaks a little louder. A little lower. Or with a different rhythm. Ask yourself if a different system than a minute ago, may be speaking through your partner in this dialogue. With a little practice, you will find it becomes easier to make the distinction between the two.

Perceiving systemically is seeing or hearing someone with the question: Which system is speaking though him or her?

Without judgment

With systemic perception, you are without judgment. You don't think anything of the situation. Judgments and opinions intervene between you and the team you want to observe. We will write more later about judgment and how you can look at this systemically.

Maybe it's easier to try to be beyond judgment. This means that you don't have to do away with your judgment, absolutely not. You accept your judgments to a great degree. Then they won't try to keep catching your attention so much when you are reflecting on your team and organisation around them.

Without intention

Systemic perception is perceiving without needing to do anything. Without having to solve anything. Without doing anything. Systemic perception is all about being. Not about doing. Difficult? But maybe liberating for a while too.

Using your body

What bodily reactions do you have with what you hear and see? Stomach ache, lightheadedness, heaviness, goosebumps? Tension in your head or shoulders that wasn't there before? Maybe it wants to tell you there is a systemic charge going on.

It took me a while to find out that my body was telling me things about what was happening 'outside' me. When I had a sudden headache, I would contribute it to a busy day, or my stiff shoulders would make me wonder what exercise at boot camp we had done to cause it, it was probably muscle ache. Sometimes it is but more often these signals mean that something in your environment, in the conversation, the meeting is changing. That something in the story, in the context of the whole, touches a pattern, something that wants to expose itself. Now, if I combine my bodily signals with what I see, hear and know about the other and make it explicit, it usually brings new information about the system to light.

Barbara Hoogenboom

As a team leader, I often behave the same way a detective does. That was easiest when I started this job. I 'took up' office on my first day as a detective who, as Jan Jacob Stam calls it, investigates the crime scene. What stands out? What comes at you? What are, as it were, the possible traces for what happened and an indication of what is ahead. I have now made it a habit when I start a new position somewhere, to take photographs of possible traces /clues over the course of the first week and write a short summary about it. Later, I can always access it when needed. Especially when I find myself stuck or drawn into the organisational system of my workplace and have become a part of. The longer I work somewhere, the harder it becomes to play detective and I now use those moments immediately after a

M.L.

> *holiday or after I have followed another systemic course, to play detective all over again.*

L.B.   *During one of the courses, the concept of 'looking without judgment', was particularly eye-opening for me to be able to continue working with a few of my employees. I was finding my ego would get in the way of those relationships because of their daily victim-mentality, showing up in their behavior, at least from my point of view. By going into the office, the next day and being in the space without judgment and letting reality come towards me, all I felt was dedication to what was happening in the interaction between employees. It created a flow for me where I could continue working together energetically with all the members of my team. At moments where I feel irritation, I now experience 'looking without judgment', also as a form of self-therapy to regain a constructive mode of operation.*

2.5.2 Not-Knowing

Not-Knowing is a part of systemic perception. For a manager this may be disastrous, not-knowing, and also for a control-freak. Let us add something to that: The Not-Knowing, with Capitals.

If you know it immediately, that then is in the way of systemic perception. You can no longer see what is presenting itself to you, but you see your reaction to that which is presenting itself.

The now-knowing precedes systemic perception. It slows down. It feels uneasy, especially if you have a set diary to follow. But if you want to do something different than your default response to a problem, you won't escape making friends with the not-knowing. Moreover, not just doing it for and within yourself but before your entire team.

> **I Don't Know**
> **I Have No Idea**
> **I Don't Know**
> **I Have No idea**

CHAPTER 2. WHAT IS 'SYSTEMIC' ALL ABOUT?

I train Human Resource managers at municipalities to deal with all changes that are coming towards them. This happens in blocks. During the intake, I always say that I have reached my goal if someone during the course of the training says that they no longer know. Everyone always gives me that look of surprise. It often happens hallway through the course when one after the other stops knowing anything anymore. The results are sometimes astonishing. Someone decides to stop working at the municipality because that isn't where her heart lies. Or someone decides to take a sabbatical year to finally make time to do something they have always wanted to do. Or one of the Human Resource advisors finally makes it to the managers table, because she only did what he asked her to do.

I.O.

The nice thing is, the more you allow others not to know, the more the system, the whole will start helping you. In a way, you abuse the fact that the system wants to be complete and also wants flow. Not-Knowing creates a void. And a void creates space. Space that wants to be filled. In Japanese, there is a word for it: 'Ma'. You could translate 'Ma' with something to the extent of 'meaningful emptiness'. It's the space in a beer glass. Not the glass itself, but the space inside it. And it wants to be filled, doesn't it?

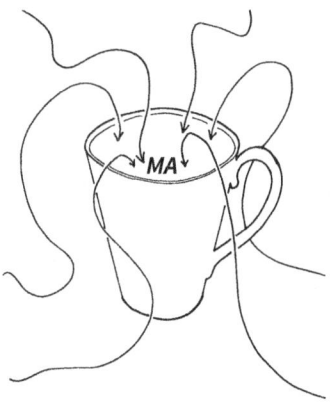

To surrender to Not-Knowing, creates a void that wants to be filled with ideas, impulses and insights.

If, as a leader in a team meeting, you truly Do Not Know, and say that out loud, it will help the meeting. Not necessarily the individuals, but the meeting as a whole. It's called co-creating. That is different to working together. When you work together, it is the sum of individuals that together form an idea or a product. Every part contributes. With co-creating it's the whole that is at work. And because the whole behaves differently than the sum of individuals, it could be that you have completely different solutions than would have been possible with the sum of individuals.

Jan Jacob Stam

We are on a long walk with four entrepreneurs. Of course, our inspiring conversation are increasingly about our companies and we lose our way to the car. We come to a 5-fork in the country roads and come to a halt when we realise that we have lost our way. We look at each other. What now? Which way? I don't know. The others don't either… One of us has a GPS but before she gets a chance to check it, one of the others says: "What if for once, we really don't know…?". One of the others immediately says: "Oh, but thén I know, we should go that way". As we check the GPS, it proves he was right. We repeat this 'procedure' at least twice and soon we arrive at the car.

2.6 Three Survival Mechanisms

The three mechanisms described below are the foundation for the phenomenological way of working. It is essential to have a clear understanding of these mechanisms to be able to understand and get a good felt sense of what an organisational system needs of leadership.

Here, we want to reflect on the people who were at the forefront of this form of systemic phenomenological work: Bert Hellinger. Anton Stuitberg Hellinger was born in 1925 near Heidelberg, Germany and at the time this book was written, he is, at 91 years old and still busy working at seminars all over the world.

CHAPTER 2. WHAT IS 'SYSTEMIC' ALL ABOUT?

The most important contribution of Bert Hellinger in his search for 'The Science of Human relations' form the three survival mechanisms that are at work in families, organisations and societies.

Hellinger discovered this through thousands of so-called constellations and as many questions on life from clients who came to seek his advice. Hellinger called these mechanisms the three consciences. Very phenomenologically, he temporarily set aside everything he already knew about consciences through various psychological movements. He started all over again, without any preconceived ideas or images, without wanting to find anything even. Often, his insights would be unexpected. He would sometimes know that something was missing in those insights yet he tried not to fill in the gaps. He endured. Hellinger is a man with an enormous discipline. As a young boy at the seminary, he was exposed to a Spartan way of life. Maybe it stems from there.

He considers his insights around the three mechanisms to be a gift. Not something constructed. How these three mechanisms work exactly, remains to be an 'ongoing development'.

The more we are starting to understand the three mechanisms, the more it becomes clear that it's about an old instinctive survival mechanism. Possibly from the time we humans used to live in herds, tribes or groups. These survival mechanisms seem inherent to the human species, although we do find them amongst horses, dogs, cows and possibly other herd animals.

Understanding the three mechanisms is at the heart of the systemic approach. Our navigator with systemic organisational issues, is the map of the three consciences. Actually, they are three different maps and we often need to switch between the three.

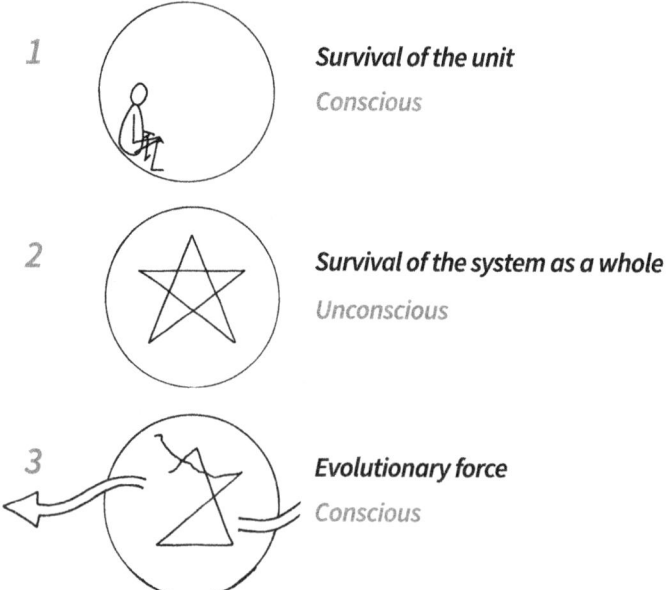

The survival mechanisms in systems.

The first mechanism takes care of the survival of the individual in a unit.
The second mechanism takes care of the survival of the herd, of the system as a whole.
The third mechanism takes care of the development and end of societies as a whole.

Within the three mechanisms there are certain rules, principles at work: in this book, we call them workings. The workings between the mechanisms are about:

- being complete & belonging
- your own place & order
- exchange in taking and giving
- destination & (de)finiteness

In chapter 3 of this book, the workings within the survival mechanisms

CHAPTER 2. WHAT IS 'SYSTEMIC' ALL ABOUT?

will be comprehensively addressed. And mainly about what this asks of leadership.

2.6.1 Survival of the individual (unit-conscience)

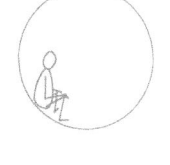

This conscience, this mechanism, serves the survival of an individual in a unit. But it is also about the survival of the unit (team, department, organisation, country) within a larger unit. It works the way one of our sense would, óne of which you are conscious.

Simply put: if, as a child, you don't know how to belong to your family unit or extended family, it's hard to survive. If, as a child, you don't know which place in the order you have, you could be kicked out and it is difficult to survive. If, as a child, you don't know how to exchange, you won't get any food or other essentials to survive. The capacity to belong somewhere or to take the right place in the order and the capacity to exchange are of vital survival-importance. That goes for individuals in a family setting as well as for organisations, in teams and other social contexts.

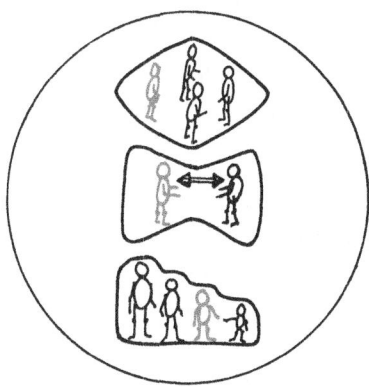

The unit-conscience has the following aspects: belonging, exchange and order.

To turn a group into a safe unit, it is useful and often necessary to exclude certain people or events. The more you pick on another team that works directly before or after you in the operations, the more the other team will feel like a unit. With the risk of becoming an island.

After a significant event, such as an employee being fired on the spot, it is nice for the cohesion of the team to either not talk about it at all anymore or to talk about it with a great deal of judgment. It's a good thing he or she doesn't belong with us anymore!

M.L. *When I started my job as team leader, I could immediately feel that the previous team leader was still around. I knew that the previous team leader had been fired. Let's call him John. When I got to my desk, it seemed as if it was taken. After I had cleared out and given everything a new place in the office, I noticed that employees would mention him without using his name. I kept thinking of the Harry Potter movies where Voldemort is never called by his name but 'he who mustn't be named'. By not calling him by his name, he seemed to be all the more present. During the first team meeting, I asked if we were complete. People nodded but were moving around uncomfortably on their seats. I took a deep breath (because it's still exciting doing a systemic intervention, I risked not belonging anymore) and said: "I think we are missing someone... John".*

At that moment, I threw some shoe soles into the group (I have a habit of having things like shoe soles, magnets and such with me). The whole team was holding their breath. One person carefully asked me what I was doing. I explained that it felt as if he was Still here and that I would rather bring someone in, in the end he wás their team leader whom they worked with for quite a while. People sighed deeply.

We looked at it together discussed if and how we still needed to could say goodbye to John. Everyone ended up saying their goodbyes in his or her own way. The strange sentence that occurred to me was: he was free and we were too.

A different example is of a leader had given his the organisation a certain signature and was fired by the director. Employees who stopped talking about the previous leader in fear of offending the present director and or leader.

Excluding people, gossiping etc., contributes to the survival mechanism of the individual in the unit, it has a very useful function. The unit-conscience tells you about the do's and don'ts of the team or organisation that you work for. The unit-conscience works directly, like one of your senses. It is in our conscious part. This, contrary to our next survival mechanism, the system-conscience.

2.6.2 Survival of the system as a whole (system conscience)

The task of the System conscience is to ensure the survival of the herd, group, organisation or system. And to help the herd, as a group, survive, this conscience sacrifices individuals to the continued existence of the system.

You can compare the system-conscience with a history book. The history book wants to record all the facts of history. If we find part of our history too painful, or we feel threatened by it, we tear out that page of our history. Yet the history book 'wants' the complete history! In the examples of the last paragraph about firing the leader and the employee, this survival mechanism will make sure that the torn pages, will be brought back into the picture. One way this could happen is that present and/or future generation of employees start showing (unconscious!) behaviour that leads to exclusion. Or that 'looks' like the behaviour of the fired people.

The previously discussed unit-conscience works unconsciously. You can feel, at any given moment, if your actions result in you belonging more or belonging less to the unit. The system-conscience, however, is unconscious by nature. What is important is that the unit-conscience often works contra productive to the system-conscience and vice versa. And: the system-conscience is often stronger than the unit-conscience.

The system-conscience creates patterns to ensure the survival of the system as a whole.

Example

When in a nursing home, a nurse abuses a resident, he will be fired on the spot and the traumatised client will be transferred to a different unit. The incident, the perpetrator and the victim are all excluded. Five years later, a young psychologist who has just been appointed in the nursing home, determines that, especially in this unit, incidents of abuse continuously take place. Incidents that can't be explained given the attitude of staff or the residents. It is as if it they are overcome by it.

In this example, the nurse has crossed a line within the unit-conscience, of the boundaries of 'belonging'. It is logical for management to fire the nurse. On the grounds of the unit conscience the nurse can no longer belong. And nor can the resident. He/she was transferred. Management tries to hide the incident. Every course of action by management makes sense, and no doubt with the best intentions, however systemically speaking not very wise.

This is how a pattern of incidents start in the department, big ones, small ones. Without anyone really understanding why. The incidents are continuously characterised by perpetratorship and victimisation. Sometimes, even nursing staff feel a victim because they are terrorised by some of the residents. The pattern is tough and can last a very long time.

CHAPTER 2. WHAT IS 'SYSTEMIC' ALL ABOUT?

Because of the friction between the unit-conscience (which excludes) and the system-conscience (which wants to include), patterns arise. In chapter 4 we will elaborate on a few commonly found patterns. We will discuss how they come to being, how you can recognise them and what you could possibly do about them.

2.6.3 Surviving the large flow of development (Evolutionary Force)

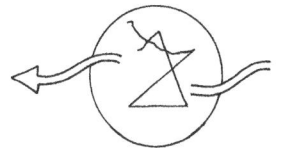

The evolutionary force is a conscience that rises above the unit-conscience and the system-conscience. It is capable of disrupting and even destroying both.

**The unit-conscience takes care
of the survival of individuals in a group.
The system-conscience takes care
of the survival of the entire system.
The evolutionary force is in service
of the greater life forces.**

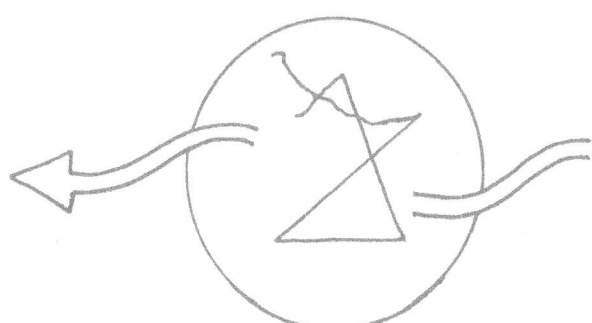

The evolutionary force blows through all systems like a storm, disrupts patterns and creates room for transformation.

It makes sure that societies as a whole develop. It creates and destroys, both without judgment. The evolutionary force creates good ánd bad, light ánd dark, peace ánd war, crisis ánd prosperity. This conscience is a vector. It is an impulse with a direction.

SYSTEMIC LEADERSHIP

This force is capable of destabilising the claws of fractals and patterns that were created under the influence of the system-conscience. The system falls, whether or not controlled, apart. If a system is destabilised enough, then from this fluid soup, new patterns can form.

The last paragraph described because of the way the system-conscience and the unit-conscience function, patterns are created in the system. Patterns that repeat themselves in more than one place and over a longer period of time.

There are many patterns in our banking system. Even though these patterns are regularly given a new face with every new bank that comes into being or with every new government regulations: in essence, the patterns are the same. Although, they could be destructive for individuals, patterns keep the system in place. The system-conscience creates fractals, continuously repeating patterns of different sizes. This system-conscience is stronger than the individuals in them. How many people will have started a job in banking, convinced that they would do things differently than their predecessors had done?

We were curious if the banking crisis in 2008 was strong enough to blow up the patterns in the sector, giving room for new patterns to evolve. By now, many years later, it looks very much like this didn't happen.

Technological and Societal developments

Technological development also belongs to evolutionary forces. Technically, as much as possible is developed, with the logical result that much doesn't need to exist anymore. New technological possibilities create redundancy.

It wasn't so long ago that every street corner had a phone booth. The phone booth had reached her destination. Not because of the lack of functionality, but because something more accessible became possible.

And technological development fosters societal development. Because of new opportunities, people start embracing different forms of

CHAPTER 2. WHAT IS 'SYSTEMIC' ALL ABOUT?

communicating shopping and working. With all its implications for existing organisations.

Organisational systems want to contribute something to the bigger picture, to society. Once, they started out for a reason, to achieve something. They have a destination, which can be very different to a mission or vision. And suddenly, or not so suddenly, a system can have reached its destination.; because great evolutionary forces like was or a crisis arise or because other innovations make your destination 'superfluous' or 'reached'. The concept 'phone booth' achieved its destination.

If you look at organisations through the lens of *"Has the destination been reached?"*, you can look differently at for example the retail industry, where chains are collapsing one by one. Or the developments in telecommunications or postal services.

The workings of the evolutionary force often translate into the question of destination. Some people refer to this as the 'personal mission' or a 'higher purpose'. We often ask entrepreneurs: *"How much destination does your company need?"* To our surprise, entrepreneurs answer that question without any hesitation. *"20 years"*, they could say. Sometimes, the organisation hasn't yet reached its destination but the entrepreneur himself has. It is good to make that distinction.

How much destination does your organisation need?
What does it still need to do, to reach in society?

At a personal level

At a personal level, people often feel the working of the evolutionary forces very well. It has to do with your life's path. And although many people are curious about or searching for their life's path, you weren't given any directions at birth. However, when you are in tune with your life's path, you are generally satisfied, calm and see the future brightly. When you are not nót in tune with your life's path, you are restless, can't seem to find your feet, you don't quite know what you want to do with your life, or better said, you don't know what life wants from you.

And sometimes there are periods in your life where you feel in tune and then suddenly or gradually, you feel that it is no longer so. You could start feeling restless or dissatisfied, not quite understand why you feel the way you do or why you are stressed out, even though you aren't busier than normal.

Then ask yourself, how much destination you still need in your present function or role. How much destination does the organisation need? Is it tuned-in? id not, it might be time to leave?

Barbara Hoogenboom

I worked in the financial sector for various large multinationals for eleven years, first in Amsterdam, then in The Dutch Antilles and Aruba and then back in Amsterdam. At my last employer, we were going through some heavy weather and even though I had 'survived' many a restructuring, I found myself starting to wonder what job I would apply for if I got fired. I would look at ads of similar functions in the banking and insurance sector. And I felt a pit in my stomach, which surprised me actually.

I had no idea what I wanted. But it was increasingly clear what I didn't want, or even cóuld! Destination reached, no doubt about it!

> " *The unit conscience covers up, the system conscience exposes, the evolutionary force awakens.* "
>
> **Bibi Schreuder and Jan Jacob Stam**

2.7 The workings in survival mechanisms

As announced earlier, the principles at work in survival mechanisms are:

1. completeness & belonging
2. your place & order

CHAPTER 2. WHAT IS 'SYSTEMIC' ALL ABOUT?

3. exchange in taking & giving
4. destination & (de)finiteness

We mainly encounter the first three workings in the unit and system conscience. The fourth working is mainly found in the evolutionary mechanism.

2.7.1 In the Unit conscience

Completeness, truly including everything (belonging)

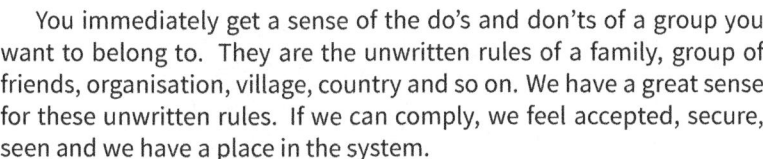

If, as a child, you don't know how to belong to your family unit or parents, it is hard to survive.

You immediately get a sense of the do's and don'ts of a group you want to belong to. They are the unwritten rules of a family, group of friends, organisation, village, country and so on. We have a great sense for these unwritten rules. If we can comply, we feel accepted, secure, seen and we have a place in the system.

Having a place is one of the most important conditions for us to flourish, be able to function well and to be happy. Having a place is also important in your ability to contribute to that group. And the more you can make a contribution and be seen by the group, the stronger your place will be. When you come into a new group, you may feel insecure, looked at or ignored. This insecurity can in turn lead to being even less accepted or feeling of acceptance, which makes your place more fragile.

As a teenager, I thought it was really cool to smoke. For a moment there, I convinced myself I enjoyed it, but t helped me to fit in. Especially with the cool guys, wearing ripped jeans and so on. So, I smoked along, cigarettes that I had sneakily taken from my parent's packets. That worked for a while. It worked so well, that I thought I could smoke from my bedroom window and spray my room afterwards with Cacharel (a scent I didn't like enough to wear) to hide the smell.

Barbara Hoogenboom

I can remember the pain and insecurity I felt when my mother started asking me some critical questions, and if I smoked. What made me feel cool in one group, made me feel very small in my family. I was honest about it and, maybe in a quest to continue to belong, I kept smoking the brand that my parents used to smoke. From my own pocket that is.

Here, we run into an important aspect of 'fitting in'. During your life, you are part of many different groups and systems. Count them for today, they should easily be ten. If you start counting your entire life so far, it may take you a while. Because you are part of many different groups and systems, you may run into loyalty conflicts.

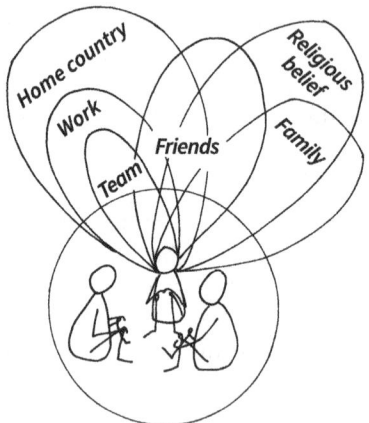

Loyalty conflicts: every system has his own norms and rules to belong. To which rules am I faithful?

Jan Jacob Stam

When I started my career at the, then prestigious, PTT Telecom, I was soon part of a program for young potentials where we were 'coloured' green. Green was the colour of the company logo and the program was a combination of orientation and socialisation. The whole idea was that we became familiar with the do's and don'ts in the organisation quickly. So that we would be adopted by the system and that we

> *would make the system our own. I knew very well that I didn't belong tóó much. Not to lose my freedom of action.*
>
> *After a few weeks, I took a risk by not following up on my boss's assignments but to look for my own way in the company. Looking back, it was a good move, because although I was almost excluded from the smaller system, my department (and I never had any problems with my boss after that point), this attitude was well appreciated in the larger system.*

If you can feel what it is you 'need' to do to belong, you also know what to do nót to belong. Of course, you can also not want to belong somewhere. The example above, illustrates that by chósing not to belong with one group, you automatically dó belong to a sub group or other part of the system.

> *I enjoy going to our holiday home on Texel, an island in the north of The Netherlands, the island is my second home. One time, our family-unit went there to play golf for the very first time. We had never been to a golf course. The golf course on Texel is beautiful and close to our holiday home. We had a lot of fun and many other golfers reacted positively to our busy children, then 4, 6 and 7 years old, who álso tried to hit a ball.*
>
> *After that, we went for coffee at the clubhouse. Startled, I suddenly saw a news sticker with required dress code. I can't remember the details but I do recall the shirt with collar. We were wearing t-shirts, sneakers and jeans and not a collar in site. My first reaction was: oops, let's go out and get some polo-shirts for all of us for next time. And after that I thought, or maybe I shouldn't!? By the way, my mother thinks I should definitely adapt to the prescribed dress code. My father feels the opposite; I should definitely nót adapt to the norm, because "we are non-conformists". Anyhow, we still go for some golf there regularly. Sometimes, I will wear a polo-shirt (yes, bought it) sometimes I won't. The best solution is to júst fit in everywhere.*

Barbara Hoogenboom

Everything has its own place / position (order)

The previous working, actually says: *"you belong if you conform to the norm of the group"*. This working says that by belonging, you dó have an own place that has to be logical with the order. Within the unit conscience you can feel how the order works.

Barbara Hoogenboom

My first real job was with an insurance company. Of the 3000 employees, 600 were fired because of the upcoming changes and 200 new, young, entrepreneurial potentials were hired. In the 'Collective Pensions' department, as a group of 12 newbies, we were locked up for 6 weeks to learn the ropes. After that, we were divided into the different teams. I can still feel and see the eyes of my new colleagues, when I sat myself down at my new desk at the far end of the office. Know that you know 'nothing'. Know that there were people fired for you. Know that you are last in line.

And at the same time, the encouraging words from my team leader and his manager, their hopeful glances about what I should be bringing to the organisation. Who may have wanted for me to be the first in line, not the last.

This example is about the principle of order in seniority over the years worked in the organisation. You could also sense a different order going on: was this insurer a more administratively run organisation – 'every policy perfect and predictable' - or was 'entrepreneurship, creativity and flexibility' what was necessary for the organisation in this phase?

In organisations, there are always multiple orders active at the same time. And, to make it easy, these different principles in the order each know their own order.

An organisation thrives when, for every person, every function, every team, every department and every business unit there is a reliable place in the framework of the organisation. Reliability in the sense that there isn't any doubt or discussion around where we belong in the system. This is a matter of effectivity and efficiency. All energy that goes towards the question: "*Where do we belong in this framework*", can't be used for exchange, productivity and thus for systemic turnover. And a lot of energy can go to this question where you belong in the order. Debilitating! Think about how this is in your family or in your work at this moment? How much energy is going towards this question? Can you guess? If more than 20% of your or your teams' energy goes into the question of order, from a systemic leadership perspective, it's a good reason to intervene!

After a major change, it is understandable that it will take some time before a new order is found. After a reorganisation or merger, it could take even a year. However, if it takes two years or more, then something is up. Another reason to intervene with some systemic wisdom.

There are four principles or order in an organisation. In order of decreasing influence:

1. Order in leading principles
2. Order in functions
3. Order in the contribution to the survival of the organisation
4. Seniority

1. Order in leading principles

This is by far the most important principle of order: leading principles are answers to the question: what in essence are we to society?

In a hospital, the medical principle could come first and the nursing principle in service of the medical principle. In a nursing-home this can be the other way around: first the nursing principle and the medical principle supporting it.

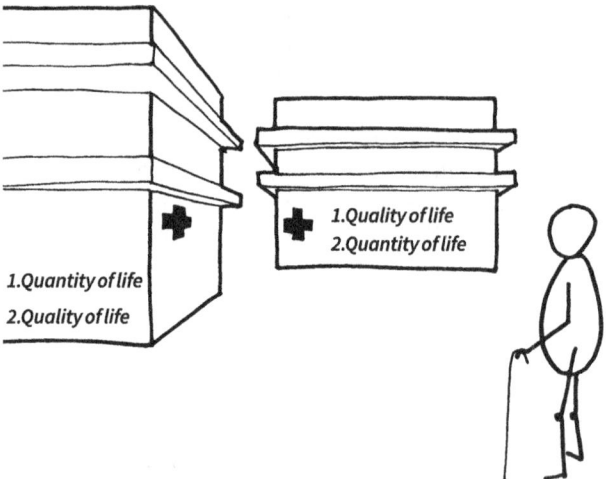

Where do I want to be? In the hospital where the quality of life comes first or in the hospital where the quantity of life comes first?

Often, there are more leading principles active in an organisation. A leading principle is not necessarily the same as a vision or mission. A mission or Vision often has a more construed character. Leading principles already exist. You áre and dó it already. Maybe they haven't always been made explicit. It can be very interesting to make them explicit, to put them in order of importance, and maybe even make them compatible with your mission and vision.

Barbara Hoogenboom

During my days as a mediator, I was called into a conflict where parents had initiated a living situation for their adult children, who weren't capable of living by themselves. A handful of your adults lived in a big house together and a team of professional staff surrounded them there. There was dissatisfaction about how things were going and one of these was about how the healthcare professionals involved family members around preparing meals. What turned out: there was confusion around one of the most basic leading principles. Was it to teach these young adults how to independently go shopping with a limited budget and learn how to make a healthy meal all the same? Or was it to teach these young adults what healthy nu-

> *trition was and that they can prepare those meals with fresh, unprocessed ingredients. The answer determines how a health care professional will use their time with the young adults to teach them what they need to learn.*

Another vivid example are elementary schools in a village or city area. Most primary schools will have the leading principle to prepare children for secondary school. And other than that, they may be the extension of parental upbringing? And maybe they contribute to the social cohesion of the area? Maybe they feel responsible for the well-being of the child?

The problem isn't that there are more than one leading principles. The problem is often that there is no clarity around which principles comes before the other. It has a direct impact on how you define the functions/roles of the employees and even what kind of employees you need.

> *Sometimes leading principles are translated into company values. Once, I worked for a spiritual centre that described themselves in a few key words: energy, honesty, real, contemporary. Take a moment to digest and feel what the effect of these words, in this particular order, have on you. What do you think? Does this centre suit you? Appeal to you? Now, turn around the order of the words: contemporary, real, honest, energy. How does it make you feel now?*
>
> *Neither order makes them better than the other but you may attract completely different clients!*

Barbara Hoogenboom

2. Order in functions

If the order of the leading principles is clear, you know which functions are necessary. This determines the order in functions.

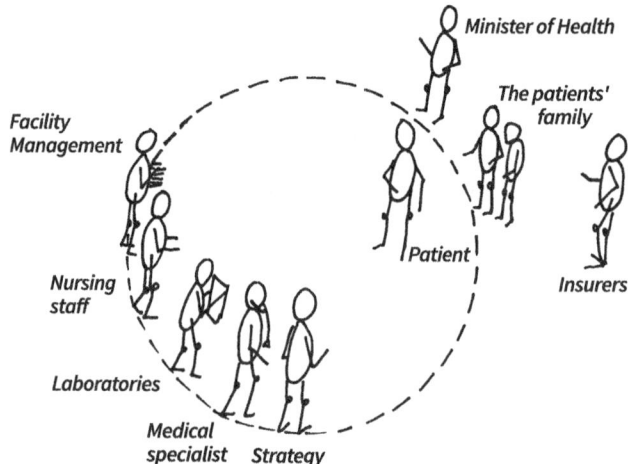

Order in functions: clockwise from more Agency (strategy, positioning) to more Communion (facilities, working together) gives a solid and reliable systemic structure.

- The functions responsible for positioning the organisation in society, the strategic functions, the functions that take care of sufficient autonomy in the system, come first. These functions are often outwardly focused and define the boundaries of the organisational system. This is what we are, and this is what not.

- In second place are the core functions of the organisation. Think of teachers (at a school), doctors (in a hospital), the baker (at a bakery chain), the policeman/woman (with the police department).

- Only then, the supporting functions follow. And the functions focused on the well-being of the organisation. In these functions, there is more inward orientation to make sure the core functions can perform their tasks.

Every function is equally needed in the whole even if in our society, the more strategic functions are rewarded better.

CHAPTER 2. WHAT IS 'SYSTEMIC' ALL ABOUT?   51

3. Contributing to the survival of the organisation in the whole

A person or department who is responsible for an accomplishment resulting in the survival of the organisation, is often experienced as higher in the order. How do you acknowledge someone who saved the company for going bankrupt, appropriately? For example, a car salesman who manages a large new order in one go? If you thank this someone fully for the merit he brought, you are certain that she or he will never feel 'normal' amongst co-workers again. If you don't give it special attention, that too will cause dissatisfaction and result in questions from the team and the person at hand.

There is often an art to finding a more or less appropriate balance in giving acknowledgement for a special contribution.

Below, you can read an example of how different kinds of orders in a team: seniority and contribution to the whole, can lead to confusion and unrest.

As an executive in a fire department, we were on the verge of a reorganisation. Lately, the management team meetings were unsettled and we hardly managed any decisions. It felt like confusion. During a special afternoon meeting organised for the reorganisation, it struck me that a few of my colleagues that would normally sit in 'fixed' seats, moved to sit somewhere else. A few front men that were chosen for the reorganisation, were also part of this management team. Together, we did some exercises where we would sit down in the order of years with the fire department, years with this organisation, and most influential in the reorganisation. With the last order, many of the 'builders' were much higher in rank in the order and we could see the confusion. Some of the team members had an inner state connected to the amount of years in service, whereas other builders were already connected to the new organisation and it created opposites.

M.L.

SYSTEMIC LEADERSHIP

4. Seniority

Seniority can be about age, amount of years in a profession, amount of years connected to the organisation, amount of years on the team. Seniority is about length of time. Where earlier we wrote about the different orders that are active in a given organisational system, when talking about seniority, there are multiple orders at the same time. It is incredibly acknowledging and helpful to bring the various orders in seniority to light with a team.

Barbara Hoogenboom

Last year, we facilitated a training Systemic Skills to a few teams of HR advisors from a Police organisation. In one of the teams, there were obvious 'newbies' and 'veterans'. The relation became apparent after we asked them to stand in the order of the amount of years that they had worked for the organisation. If, by the way, you want to be impressed by something, try looking at the years of service at a Police organisation! Except for the veterans there were a few people that had only been with the police for a few months.

When they continued to sit in the order of amount of years in the business of HR, it turned out that many of the 'newbies' had a lot of experience in HR. They were hired as external experts for this period of time. Some of the 'veterans' were new to the business of HR. They had chosen a different job to the core function they had had before. The looks and words everyone shared gave a lot of acknowledgement.

One of the HR staff was a woman who had been in the most senior position twice. She could tell everyone a vast amount about the development of this (HR) area at the Police. She told the group that she had had to step out of service when she got married because in the old days, a married woman had to stop working.

Honesty in taking and giving (exchange)

They sometimes say that there should be a balance in giving and taking. However, if there is a balance, that would mean standing still. Better, or livelier, is when there is a permanent imbalance in taking and giving. And there is a fine line in the imbalance: not too much or too little, otherwise the mechanism doesn't work.

CHAPTER 2. WHAT IS 'SYSTEMIC' ALL ABOUT?

When my children were very young, my husband and I often needed a babysitter for a few hours. For instance, to take care of the youngest while I took the toddlers swimming. A friend of mine offered to do it. And she didn't want anything for it in return. It didn't feel right: in my busy life of that moment, I wouldn't be able to do anything for her in return. I insisted paying her otherwise I couldn't ask her with a clear conscience.

Barbara Hoogenboom

The mechanism is simple: If someone gives you something, you feel the pressure to do something in return. If that something is a little more than you had been given in the first place, the other person in turn feels pressure to give something back to you, possibly resulting in a lively exchange. The more exchange, the more liveliness.

This works the other way around as well. If someone did something to you, you may feel you are in your right to retaliate. If that is more than was initially done to you, that's a good start for an escalation, revenge or war.

A solution to this spiral is the so-called 'revenge with love': requiring something from the other, but just slightly less than what was done to you. Then, the balance can be restored or can we begin with a clean slate and start again.

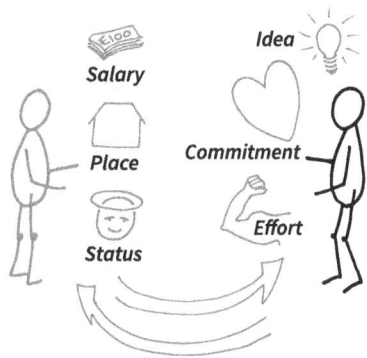

Letting talents flow freely requires a fair exchange in taking and giving between adults or equals.

SYSTEMIC LEADERSHIP

This mechanism of exchange works the same in organisations. And not only in terms of money or turnover. Other than an income, an organisation offers employees security, maybe status, a place where your talents can come to fruition and so on. In turn, employees offer their talents, time, commitment and reliability, creativity, sweat and passion. There is an exchange of taking and giving inside the organisation as well as between the organisation and the outside world.

The organisation delivers products and services. The clients or sometimes society – in case of subsidised institutions – pay. They don't merely pay in money, but also by repeatedly, connecting to the organisation each time you buy a product, however brief.

M.L. *One of the most difficult and beautiful aspects of my work is talking to an employee and discovering that his or her talent has stopped moving. If it can't keep flowing in the organisation, it could mean that his or her destination at this organisation has been reached. That is also a little unnerving because, who am I to say this? I have discovered that if I say it from my functions position – my place in the organisational system – and not from me as a person, it works better. Once, I worked with an employee who had worked for the organisation for decades. He had had many different functions: management positions. It was hard for him and it never worked out. After the reorganisation three years ago, he ended up in a specialist job. When I looked at him, it was as if he pulled a ball and chain behind him. Figuratively speaking, I could see his scars.*

At first, I thought systemic coaching could be useful for him. I was right to a certain extent because it would allow him to unlock a new source inside himself. At the same time, he realised that his older talents were put out or exhausted. And that possibly, his new source couldn't find ground here. 'Time to go': I said and yes it hurt. As a systemic leader, I feel obliged to shine light on sources and talents. When they flow and when they no longer do.

What happens when you give your employees too much? When the imbalance in taking and giving has become too big. If you give them more than is in agreement with what they can give back in performance. Then they become smaller and feel like children. At some stage, they will then have to leave. A long-lasting imbalance in giving and taking is intolerable. The atmosphere will become depressed and exchange dries up. Sooner or later, people will go their separate ways.

For a time during my professional life as a mediator, I was an enthusiastic member of the board for the trade association for mediators. I spent many an hour working on this. Hours and effort that I couldn't put into my paid work as a mediator or in my own marketing activities. I had a wonderful time with the other members and it enlarged my network and gave me some status, but it didn't have an influence on my bank account.

I only came to realise how big the imbalance was until after I left. Every time I was asked for an unremunerated function, I kept declining: it was someone else's turn to give their time and passion.

Barbara Hoogenboom

How big should a (micro) credit be to give maximum growth potential? If it's too big, the person involved will be eternally stuck to the lender and in a sense, becomes an employee of the lender, or worse, a serf.

What is the right amount for people receiving government benefits? When do benefits truly help you through a difficult patch in your life and when do the benefits oblige the person receiving it, to remain victim and ill?

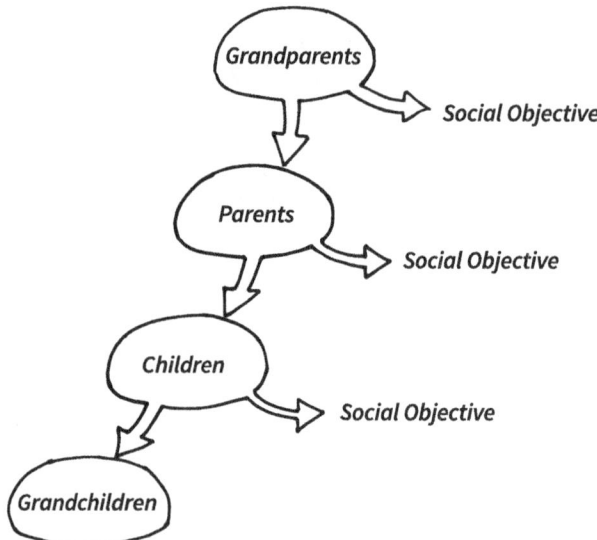

In a family system, parents give and children take. That is an essentially different feeling than the exchange between equals.

Essentially, exchange within families is different than between adults in organisations. Parents give and children take, starting with life itself. Because children can't give back 'Life' to their parents, they pass it on to their own children or to some societal goal. So, through family systems, a vertical flow of giving and taking runs across generations.

Consider to what extent your organisations behaviours resemble family traits and what the consequences are? Who belong more and who less? What is more possible and what is less?

2.7.2 Within the System-Conscience

Completeness, truly including everything (belonging)

Exclusion

Exclusion is saying that something or someone no longer belongs, that something isn't allowed to be complete anymore. We no longer speak

CHAPTER 2. WHAT IS 'SYSTEMIC' ALL ABOUT?

of that incident, those employees who were fired, that terrible company policy we had years ago, that clown of a manager who, thank goodness, left the organisation, that depressed building we worked in for over forty years.

For the unit-conscience this can be useful. However, the system-conscience doesn't allow for this and manages that the behaviours that are being excluded, reappear later or somewhere else in the organisation. This leads to all sorts of patterns (about which you can read more in chapter 4) and to all sorts of symptoms such as unconscious resistance, excessive judgments, absenteeism, conflicts and more.

Everything has its own place/position (order)

The system-conscience is unforgiving as it settles a breach in the order. This happens in three different ways.

1. Firstly, it's about time, in the way the order came to being. Wanting to improve or undo what a previous generation delivered, however awful, is doomed to failure. A simple rule of thumb can be: new comes before old, with respect for the old.

2. Secondly, it is about the place in the order of the organisation. Opposing leadership, against the very people who have made it possible that you can work here, is also doomed to fail. Unless you apply and are hired, for a function as boss of your boss.

3. Thirdly, it is about leading principles. If it isn't clear which leading principle precedes the next, it will evolve into an issue that will seep into all layers of the organisation.

Honesty in taking and giving (exchange)

The system conscience is unforgiving, too, with dishonesty in taking and giving. If an organisation acquires wealth at the expense of others' health or happiness, then later, people will unconsciously feel that they need to pay or compensate for the dishonesty somewhere else in the system. The ruthlessness of it, is that the mechanism, as all mechanisms pursuant to the system-conscience, is unconscious. It feels more as if it happens to you more than that you are actively doing it.

Barbara Hoogenboom

In Latvia, a CEO of an indoor and outdoor advertising company, wanted to explore why all her predecessors were fired from the company due to fraud? Employees stole from the company too. She didn't want to follow this pattern. When we looked for the source, the 'systemic reason', for the fraud in a constellation, it appeared that the organisation was still connected to a certain time-period (1944 – 1991) where the Soviets had usurped Latvia. During this period, all possessions were confiscated, family members murdered, many lives were upset in many different ways. After this period, many international investors came to Latvia. Even though they were responsible for giving the economy the necessary impulse, these investors took good care of their own 'wallets' too. The theft had to make amends in the balance of taking and giving. Moreover, the question is, how many more years will theft be 'necessary' if the history of Latvia isn't acknowledged. The Soviets as well as the Latvians don't speak about it anymore.

In chapter 4, the chapter on Patterns, we will elaborate on the consequences if one of the workings of the system is in a fix.

2.7.3 Within the Evolutionary Force

Destination and Finiteness

Destination is related to finiteness. Something can be finished. In family system, this notion of finiteness is hardly present. Yes, people die, lives end. But we don't think of a family system in terms of being finished or that it will end. The notion of finiteness is something we don't inherit from our family system.

Because the evolutionary force is always at work, societies change, sometimes in shocks, it could also be that smaller systems within the bigger system, come to an end.

To our surprise, participating school leaders attending an introductory afternoon about systemic work, were mainly interested in the question if the current educational system had reached its destination. Many

CHAPTER 2. WHAT IS 'SYSTEMIC' ALL ABOUT?

of the questions we get from local governments is the questions: *"Has the concept of government, as we have known it for so long, reached its destination?"*.

In our changing society, it strongly looks like many concepts, that have served us for decades or even millennia, are possibly coming to an end.

Millennia? Yes, sometimes that is what it looks like. What we have seen in our current health care system is that there is a deep and hidden systemic sentence: If I can help you, Í feel better'. When this pattern revealed itself again, Hellinger stepped forward and said: *"It is a deeply rooted Christian movement: if I help you, I feel better. It is what our health care system is built on"*. Could it be that this deeply rooted pattern has reached its sell by date? Moreover: this systemic sentence in health care gives a good reason why the system of health care is growing faster than the need for health care.

And what do we do when something has reached its destination? When something is finished, done. Our natural inclination, possibly because we don't think in terms of finiteness in family systems, is too continue for as long as possible. And many organisations are transformed.

Over the course of the last decade in the last century, I worked on many consultancy projects in Housing Cooperatives. They were brought to life after World War 2 to create cheap housing for the poor. That task was fulfilled at the end of the century. Many Housing Cooperatives, transformed into developers or speculators. In itself, this isn't good or bad. But sometimes, it is more powerful to just end something. And to use this power to create something new.

Jan Jacob Stam

Ending something also means consciously letting something go. Without knowing what will come in its place. And that is the core of transformation. With transformation we mean, entering into a process where you acknowledge that what's done is done and it consciously stops and doesn't die a slow death. And that you don't yet know what will replace it. If the concept of a City Council has reached its destination, then the terrifying part of transformation is that we don't know what will come in its place.

Emerging Future

The emerging future. The future as it is approaching us. If we like it or not. The emerging future doesn't always look a pretty picture. The evolutionary force and the emerging future aren't the same yet cast from the same mould.

> NB: The Emerging Future is a term from Gœthe, later used as an important concept in the Theory-U. Otto Scharmer, author of Theory-U, introduced the concept Emerging Future. But he used it in a different way than we do in the systemic context. Otto Scharmer used the notion as a friendly, wanted form of a future in a better world. From a systemic perspective, this use of the term Emerging Future lies closer to the 'planned future'.
>
> The term 'emerging future' that we use, lies closer to Hellinger's notion of 'Geist' or 'Spirit Mind'. In Dutch, we translated this concept into 'Geest', but this term is alien to the world of organisations. So, we use 'emerging future' differently than Otto Scharmer. Because Otto Scharmer introduced the concept earlier than we did, we have disregarded the 'intellectual property'.

CHAPTER 2. WHAT IS 'SYSTEMIC' ALL ABOUT?

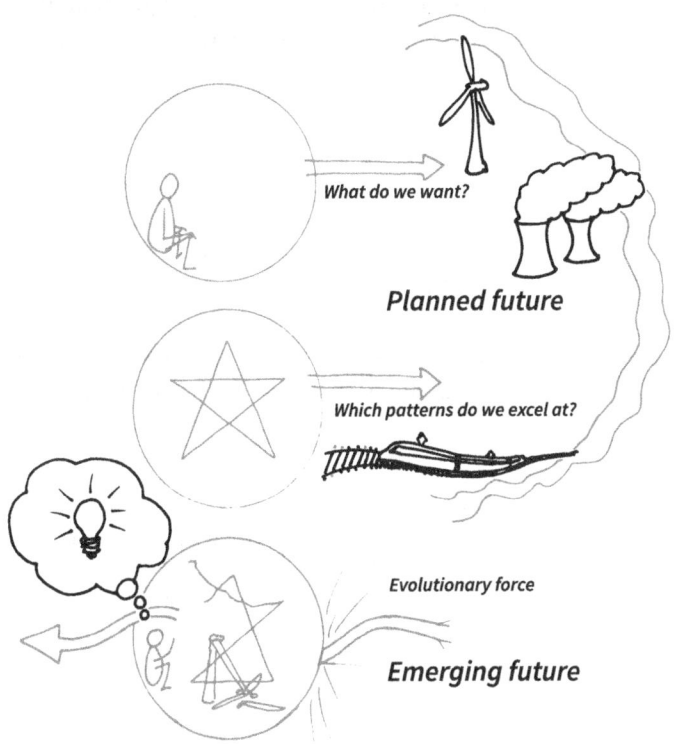

We build the planned future before us like a safe embanked landscape. The emerging future approaches us, creating as well as destroying.

Organisations, and most people, often have a planned future. Those are our plans, the goals of an organisation, the policy in society etcetera. The planned future is actually always made in a friendly way, for it is also something you want. Even if we want to destroy ourselves or a competitor, there is usually a positive intention behind it. We push the planned future forward as it were, like a wave. Maybe it makes the circle of our system bigger. The only thing we have to do is to bring in the planned future. The planned future is an outward movement.

The emerging future has the opposite direction. It approaches us. And if we look to the world around us, we see that it creates prosperity as well as crisis, war as well as peace. The emerging future has many faces. For organisations, it I an interesting question where the waves of the planned future meet the emerging future. Can we learn from the emerging future?

Emerging Past

Emerging Past is the potential and talent that was present in an organisation or person but the potential was cut off by circumstances and never used. Strangely enough, the potential is ever present and 'wants' to be seen, acknowledged and rewards reaped.

Emerging past comes into existence because there had been a dramatic, disruptive event in the past. An accident, a bankruptcy, a crisis, war etcetera.

Jan Jacob Stam

My mother desperately wanted to study French but because the university closed as the second world war started, that possibility was cut off for her. Immediately after the war, she became a mother. Her job as a mother determined the road map of her life and a university study was no longer possible. Her talent sought a way out but never came to fruition. As her son, I know her mainly as a mother.

A while ago, we did an exercise with e mini-constellation, a visualisation with representatives that made different parts of a system visible. Other than my mother and war, I could also 'see' her potential and talent for French. Even though my mother passed away years ago, her potential seemed alive and kicking. In fact, as her son, I could connect to that potential. Not make it my own or steel it, because you can't be the owner of potential. Potential wants something with you. But I could feel the family fortune of the potential of my mother well. It had two effects: the first thing being that I could now see my mother more as a woman with all the potential she had, more than in her role as a mother who had wanted to study French but couldn't. Secondly, my pleasure in French has increased.

Generally, dramatic events in an organisation lead to division. Division between those who get to stay and those who had to leave. Those

CHAPTER 2. WHAT IS 'SYSTEMIC' ALL ABOUT?

who are successful and those who lose. Perpetrators and victims. The good and the evil. Those who are fór and those who are against. The precise and the compromising. In short: one group and the other.

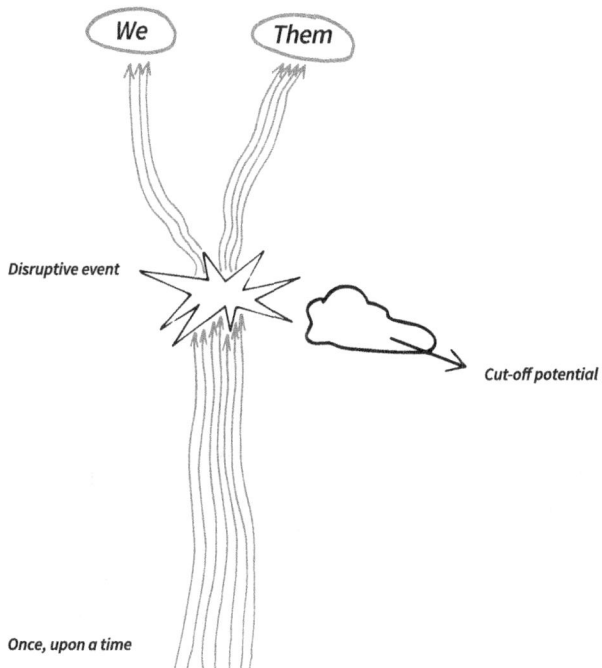

A disruptive event can cut off life-potential and that which was óne is split. Who is open to it, can re-connect with the potential that was cut off, the emerging past.

Befóre the dramatic event, everything was óne. Because of the event, the organisation or society inadvertently falls apart in sub-groups.

In the earthquake zone where I live, the world was suddenly divided in to people who caused it and victims; the ones who made the money and the ones who suffered damages. With the discovery of gas in 1959 and until the magnitude of the quakes caused major damage,

Jan Jacob Stam

there was a lot more unity. Ánd pride. It seems as if Groninger (Dutch province) have lost the capacity to be proud. And the capacity to self-repair after a natural disaster. Weren't we able to do just that for two thousand years? Self-repair? Without external millions?

Example | "In Brabant (Dutch province), there is an enormous discussion going on about large-scale livestock farming", *a process leader of this issue, who works with many of the groups involved, tells us.* "Parties want a solution but are also buried in their own position and patterns. Everyone feels that society is divided. What needs to happen for a next step to be taken. Everyone feel resistance: of course, there is loyalty to the constituency: "If I take a step in finding solutions, I may betray my constituency". This is loyalty within a group of like-minded."

However, there is also another, even more resilient loyalty. Loyalty towards the ideals with which someone started the battle, as well as loyalty to the solutions that someone has already fixed in their minds. Moving in accordance with these kind of complex transformational processes, requires being able to let go of your own ideals as well as the planned future. Not Knowing becomes the leader, and not the sum of plans.

During the process, instead of looking at the future with all parties involved, you could choose to make use of the emerging past. In the example of Brabant, and livestock farming at how society and livestock farming looked like befóre people were divided in pro and con. And you look at the potential of livestock farming at the time. And at what livestock farming meant to society. And to, if what was once possible is still present today. *"This is the wholeness that the entire province of Brabant longs for"*, one of the leaders in the process voiced.

If you want to mobilise the emerging past on your way to the future, then you don't look at the perpetrators and victims that came to being in the slipstream of the dramatic event at or period. Instead, you look at the potential and all capacities and life energy that was there before the disruptive event. You look at the united-ness and the flow that was there right before the bomb went off. Undoubtedly, the bomb served a purpose. But the side effect was that after that moment, the system was divided in pro and con. Keep in mind that all the parties that are opposing each other today all have the same origin. Acknowledging that unit, and the feeling of unity, without wanting that back, helps to let the potential of before, flow today.

To be completely clear: you want to be able to use the potential. You don't want the past back. That is forever gone.

You want to be able to tap into the pattern and from the source of the unity without wanting the unit or the solidarity of fifty years ago back. The unit of today and of tomorrow looks different to the unit of before. But they all tapping from the same source. Namely, what it means to be human. Including the shadow sides ánd the light side.

Nurturing your systemic leadership

3

It's quite something, what an organisational system requires from leadership. You probably already do much of this naturally, because people are systemically intelligent. Systemic conscience is something was ingrained in us as a child even if you never realised it. As a child, no one needed to tell you there was a family secret, you figured that out all by yourself. When your parents 'fed' you certain things, you knew if your parents had their full attention for you or if they were trying to feed something else. If attention was truly with you, you would probably 'bite' sooner than when your mother or father was trying to avoid the tension in their relationship. After all, what you avoid, is already here. You could feel it.

In this chapter, you will find the core of what a system demands of leadership.

3.1 Two basic needs of every system: autonomy and well being

We wrote about it earlier: every system is part of a bigger system. A team is part of a department. An organisation is part of the outside world. This in itself requires strong leadership.

Agency: every system needs a force that makes sure that the boundaries of a team and the positioning of the team in relation to the larger system, are clear.

CHAPTER 3. NURTURING YOUR SYSTEMIC LEADERSHIP

Every unit (team, company, family) has two basic needs: one of them is safety, security and knowing where you belong in the outside world. Ken Wilber calls this force 'Agency'. This translates well to Autonomy. Leadership must position the unit in the outside world as well as maneuver through the outside world.

Try seeing yourself as a bus driver. When you drive a school bus, it has to be clear that you aren't a commuter bus, so you won't be stopping at the bus stops where people are waiting. As a leader, you also have to guard who can and can't board the bus. If the bridge is broken, as the driver, you know you need to take a detour. Maybe you should tell parents and teachers about this too. And the swimming pool needs to know that the children will be a few minutes late today because of the detour. This is agency: when the driver makes sure that the bus is and remains a school bus, is identifiable for the outside world, and ensures of the safety of the bus as a whole. It gives confidence and clarity to the school leadership team, the parents, the swimming pool and the outside world.

Communio: every system needs a force that makes sure that well-being and cooperation within the team is possible.

The other force that requires leadership, is 'Communio', in other words connection, well-being, cohesion order and flow within the team.

Team meetings, performance reviews, eye for everyone. This communion function is even needed in teams with consultants who each have their own client portfolios.

In communion keeps your attention as a bus driver with the children in the bus. How do we keep things a little cozy and happy, even if children are being tease for their fear of water? As a bus driver, you need to be very resourceful.

It sounds simple, but what it means is that the bus driver needs to have two kinds of attention: one inwardly, in the bus, and outwardly, to bring the whole between all stakeholders, to the end goal. Attention inside ánd outside.

And the manager of the bus driver? How does he or she choose which bus driver is suited to drive from school to the pool? Does the boss think more in terms of: *"the bus needs to go from the school to the pool"*, or *"the children need to get to their swimming class"*?

Is there more attention to Agency or more for Communio? The natural preference of a team leader for more agency or more communion, can be different to what a team needs. Leadership requires to always be informed about what the team needs: more agency or more communion.

When, as the leader, you are criticized for being too 'outside' or 'inside', and they often mean that you are physically more here or there, ask yourself: where am I internally? And, when – possibly- being outside too much, what am I trying to do there? Is more agency needed? Am I unconsciously trying to restore the imbalance between agency and communion?

Take a look at your own manager or colleagues with these eyes: what is their preference in terms of agency and communion? What are they trying to do for the system: more autonomy, clear boundaries with the outside world? Or are they trying to establish more connection to each

CHAPTER 3. NURTURING YOUR SYSTEMIC LEADERSHIP

other, that everything inside works together smoothly and people are able to function properly?

In any case, it could be very refreshing to look at a manager or colleague, about whom you might even have a slight judgment, with different eyes: what is he or she trying to (unconsciously) do for our team or even for the bigger system?

Esther manages a merged government organisation: the executive bodies of some of the municipalities were merged a few years ago. From an organisational perspective, it is complex. Esther is responsible for the entire social domain. Esther seems a competent leader. I even have the impression she is working at a lower level than her qualities indicate. She tells us that now, a year after the merger, there is much confusion amongst the employees. Absenteeism is high. Esther would le to know what a first step could be towards more flow and turning the frustrated energy into energy towards the outside world.

Systemically speaking, frustration is blocked energy. So, in itself, frustration is a good sign. What is needed, is getting the bolt of the door and letting the energy flow in a certain direction.

During the constellation, we soon realise that the employees feel a deep connection to citizens who have high expectations of government. Over the course of the last year, Esther repeatedly had the tendency to look inward, to her team. Which seems logical after a merger, bringing things back into order. But if a leader has a focus inside, some part of the system nééds to have an outward focus. The simple insight for Esther is that, when she looks outside, her employees become calmer. The laughter that came to Esther when she embodied this insight, was also a liberating sort of laugh.

Seen from Agency, Esther could put more of her talents to use. The source for the work in this organisation is outside, with the citizens.

Jan Jacob Stam

Esther position is at the very edge of the team and the outside world. In a sense, she is a middle manager this way. In paragraph 3.4.2 we will go deeper into the specific systemic aspects of the middle manager.

By solely and simply changing her orientation, a whole new dynamic came into being and the beginning of a rekindled flow.

3.2 Systemic Leadership in three survival mechanisms

Every one of the three survival mechanisms, the unit conscience, the system conscience and the evolutionary force, asks for a different intervention and leadership.

The consciences, derived from the survival mechanisms, each have their own 'rules of the game'. These rules sometimes contradict each other. For some guidance, you could refer to paragraph 2.6 again.

3.2.1 The unit conscience

The unit conscience is conscious. At any moment, you can know, feel what the effect is of things that you do. For instance: do I belong more or less to this organisation, does this increase or decrease flow, do I take a more or less fitting position in the organisation. We have a sensory organ for knowing this.

Example

"How was the interview with the two candidates yesterday?"
"Well, they would be up to the task of the job. But K felt a lot more part of our little group and N a lot less."
"How do you know?"
"You can just feel it…"

Leadership requires to keep an eye out for employees' belonging. Do they have a place in the team? If they work from home, are they still present enough? Do they belong? Are they being bullied? Are there any black sheep? Do new people get enough of a chance to belong as well as bring in their own uniqueness?

Leadership keeps an eye out for employees' talents and if they are given the opportunity to flow. Are they being appreciated for their talents? Where do people work below their and where do they work above their capacities? How do I bring balance to that? And is the education I am offering them in alignment with the yet unused potential of people?

So, it is watching over the parts of the system and intervening on them.

Leadership also keeps an eye on the whole. What binds us and what separates us? What are our leading principles? Is it good to revisit them during a team meeting? And how do we deal with incidents? Are they allowed to a place in the history of the team? How do we deal with loss? Can we be disappointed about it together or do we rub it out? How do we celebrate success?

It is more about intervening on the whole here.

How much flow does the department as a whole produce? Is it time for new products and services? Is someone's voice drowning out the others or is someone laying low? Is the order in the team clear enough that everyone can trust it and build on it? Zo there is safety in the group?

Towards the outside world: does the team have a reliable place in the organisation as a whole? Where are there frictions with other teams? Is there a fuss about who comes first and who comes next? If so, does it ask for interventions that position the team clearly in the organisation as a whole? For a team leader, this usually means speaking to other colleague team leaders and with other managers.

3.2.2 The System Conscience

The system conscience asks something special from a leader. Namely, that he is or becomes aware of information and patterns that are playing an unconscious part.

This requires an open attitude, mind and necessary systemic knowledge. Systemic perception systemically is very useful and helpful. It requires the willingness to zoom out, for example to larger systems and previous events and it requires the willingness to zoom in to what is going on from the present in the bigger context.

Perceiving systemically, requires, even if it is only situational or temporary, to withhold any personal judgment. Not that you can't have judgments, because as you know, that would be a good recipe to bring in a lot of judgment. But to park your judgment systemically for a minute, in a way that you can be curious again and look at what there is more, past judgment.

What does system conscience demand of leadership?

Leadership knows the history of the organisation, knows which incidents, split-offs and mergers happened in the past, which of these events have been processed well and which still lead to 'old wounds', even if no one who lived through those events is here any longer.

Leadership can carry the burdens of these events, acknowledge them, without wanting to change them.

Leadership knows the influence patterns have on and in an organisation. These could be unconscious patterns, or have come from society or family at the time when the organisation was founded. These patterns can be productive or prohibitive.

Example

During a full day around transition in the energy branch, someone at the ministry of Economic Affairs brings an issue to the table. An issue that would turn out that she, and her division of Economic Affairs, were prepared to look at themselves. They were even prepared to face a possible transformation. At one point the question arose: "When was (this part of) Economic Affairs actually founded?" Answer: "1973". "What did society look like at the time?". "Ah yes! We had the Oil Crisis! And Economic Affairs (or this division) was founded to guarantee the delivery reliability of oil, petrol and gas. That gave a very straightforward pattern. Everything is in pursuit of

> one goal: We take care of fuel. The organisation still knows that pattern of 'unity for everything'. Even if the initial reason for the pattern was long gone! And this pattern still makes it difficult for us to look in a differentiated way".

The example of Economic Affairs perfectly illustrates how by acknowledging the start of a pattern it clears the path. Unconsciously holding on to something what was once the grounds for the raison d'être of an organisation, is no longer necessary.

Leadership knows what the overriding patterns are both within the team as well as in the entire organisation.

Leadership knows what the overriding patterns are of every employee zo she knows what kind of task or activities would go well with the employee, so their talents can flow freely.

Leadership knows what the overriding patterns are with clients and in the outside world where the organisation fulfills her task. And she knows how to grow past dysfunctional patterns.

Leadership looks at the organisation with soft eyes to find out what hidden systemic sentences the organisation or branch has. As in (Dutch) Health Care: *"If I help you, I feel better"*. These hidden systemic sentences are often the opposite of politically correct sentences. And once they have been voiced, they immediately give way to relief and space.

> *Cooperation has been one of the highest-ranking goals in a tax organisation. Despite several attempts they found unity in the teams but not in the organisation as a whole. Also, cooperating with external consultants didn't work out well. We can do it better ourselves, the prevailing thought seemed to be. The organisation know a wealth of judgments about the outside world. Because of its failure, management made the goal of cooperation bigger year. Unconsciously knowing that the feasibility of it couldn't keep up.*

L.B.

> *A constellation with the issue of why cooperation was so hard, finally gave the hidden systemic sentence "We are about you, you are not about us". A sentenced voiced to a taxpayer who fully embraced it. The teams set up in the constellation, sighed a sigh of relief. The sentence made it possible for everyone to see each other. Not just the teams amongst each other but also third parties.*

Leadership knows that resistance is a form of loyalty and rebellion a form of dedication to the system as a whole.

Leadership knows what the requirements are for change processes.

In Transformational processes, leadership is willing to develop a great wingspan for that process where we don't know where we will end up. Leadership knows that certain events can lead or have led to trauma in an organisation, not related to personal trauma of individuals; Leadership knows that often during a trauma, important traits will be (were) lost to be able to survive. Also, leadership knows how the lost traits can be regained in an organisation. Leadership looks out for (potential) future trauma that can occur as a result of decisions that have to be made.

Lastly, as a systemic leader, you álso know how difficult it is to become aware of the unconscious patterns in your system coming from the perspective outside of the system, from the point of view of the greater context. After all, you yourself are part of that system. Maybe you are also part of the problem and/or the pattern. The systemic leader is open to calling for systemic help from either a systemic-aware colleague from the bigger system or a systemic professional from outside of the organisation.

A.R.   *One of the programs at our school that is known as 'difficult', will have a new director. It is the second one in a relatively short period of time. They had an observer for a while who identified all the problems. I discuss these problems with the new director. Once we have gone through the list, I tell him something is missing. The director answers apologetically that the list is undoubtedly not complete. I answer that*

CHAPTER 3. NURTURING YOUR SYSTEMIC LEADERSHIP

what is missing is that most of these problems have been around for a long time.

The director is silent for a moment en then makes an unexpected connection. She says, she suddenly recognizes that many of these problems are the same problems in the profession this specific program leads to. A year later, most of the issues have been solved.

3.2.3 The evolutionary force

Leadership starting from the evolutionary force knows that life wants to bring forth life. This also counts for organisations and for society at large. It is about the notion that life wants something with us and with our organisation. That life wants to do something with society thróugh us and thróugh our organisation. Even if that is sometimes destroying.

Leadership that is tuned into the evolutionary force, can face what is done: the entrepreneur, the organisation, leading principles of the company, product, clients etcetera.

Amsterdam is a city in transition. Places where people used to live, become working areas, derelict terrain becomes a new residential area, water becomes land and is given a destination. As a consequence, more families with children move throughout the city, move outside and sometimes schools are forced to close due to the influx of children stopping altogether.

A.R.

This was the case with our foundation for primary education. Organising the farewell, how to do this, where understanding of systemic leadership proves to be valuable. I was sparring partner for the director who lead the process (systemically schooled himself) and I led a few sessions with the board. These sessions would be with other schools within the foundation who were also experiencing influx problems and were under pressure to learn from each other and give support where needed. With every important step in the process we did a table-constellation. This helped enormously to get the entire picture of the system that was part of the next step. The total order that needed to be adhered to in the order of action, order of decision making, order of who leads what.

To know who or what, at that moment, needed to be acknowledged most (the parents, the teachers, the children, the partnering schools, the board,…

To see the fate of every part was and where the risks lie to carry things for one another.

Looking back on the process, we can determine that, acknowledging the pain that goes with saying goodbye, everyone was able to take up a new suitable place.

Leadership knows how much potency and for how many years the organisation has left. And is prepared to, when the time comes, actively end it. Done is done.

Leadership knows where the planned future and the emerging future meet. And sometimes leadership is capable to gain insights from the emerging future and bring it into the present. Without a doubt, the founder of Apple, Steve Jobs, was capable of that.

Leadership knows what the correct moment is to answer to the future that is approaching us. It knows the Greek time God Kairos., the God of the right moment. This means that the other time god, Kronos, the one of gradual planning, needs to take a step back. Following Kairos, is intuitively knowing what is the right moment to let you take it along with it. And with all that Kronos is. In transformational processes, the emerging future is the client. Even if someone from the company or from society voices the assignment.

3.3 Completeness, including truly everything (Belonging)

One of the most important workings of survival mechanisms, is the principle of completeness, belonging. If this working is being compromised, so if (parts of) something or someone is not (or no longer) allowed to belong, or carelessly forgotten, this is the greatest cause for problems. Most patterns are in one way or another the consequence of compromising the principle of completeness.

This paragraph is about some of the subjects that touch upon the theme of completeness and belonging.

3.3.1 The origin

The first aspect of Belonging is the origin. There where it all started. For an organisation, origin could be the original idea in relation to a product or service.

For a systemic leader, it is essential to know the ins and outs of the origin of the organisation. For some organisations, for instance very old ones, often merged organisations or governments, this will be a big job. At the very least, as a systemic leader, you want to know:

- What was the reason to start this organisation?
- Who were its founders? Is or was there a founder behind the founder?
- Was there a special event that ignited the start, event along the lines of changes in legislation, economic situation, personal situation etcetera?
- What would it solve, bring, improve in society?
- What was the societal context of the time? What did the world look like at the time?
- Where did the finances come from?

It could well be that deeply rooted patterns in your organisation today, directly relate to the origins of the organisation. Over the years we have done many a constellation for organisations that proved to be built on the same event: The North Sea Floods in 1953 in Zeeland, The Netherlands. This disaster was the start for many construction and transport companies. It was also the reason the Dutch Ministry of Transport starter the Delta plan. And there is nothing wrong with starting a profitable construction business on the debris of a natural disaster, if there is acknowledgment for, for instance, the victims ánd survivors. If you make your contribution 'face to face' with and in acknowledgement of 'the horrifying tragedy'.

A.R. *The college where I work, as most of the colleges in The Netherlands, was founded after a process of merger and acquisition. The last merger was in 1993. As the third five-year anniversary in 2008 was on its way, the governing board realised that with this anniversary, they would sell the original founders as well as the rich history short. It seems that in the attic of the building, there is a painting of the original founders. They restore it and it is given a prominent place in the main conference room. This way, in 2008, we didn't only celebrate the 15th anniversary but the 210th as well.*

Personal origin

The origin is like a special force. The origin often acts as a source. Think about your own origin as a professional. Connecting to that origin makes you strong, gives you power.

Your ancestors and parents, your place of birth, country of birth, the beginning of an organisation and the moment you decided to do or learn something, all belong to your origins. The nice thing about your origins is that you take it everywhere you go irrespective of all the difficult situations that your will come up against in the course of your inevitable development.

Your origins are inalienable. It can't be taken from you. It can't be changed. It is something in you as well as around you. The origin is also the source of life itself. The good thing about source is that, however much you take from it, source will never dry up, on the contrary!

CHAPTER 3. NURTURING YOUR SYSTEMIC LEADERSHIP

Berthe's family business makes and sells fertiliser in Venezuela. Her family is scattered and at odds with each other. This started when government started seeing certain raw materials of fertilisers as drugs. Gonzalo, Berthe's brother, also one of the directors of the company, was even put in jail for it. He left the country and can't return to Venezuela. Ricardo is also a brother of Berthe and works in the company. He stayed in Venezuela to take care of his parents. To be able to do this, he embezzled money. Despite their conflict, Berthe, Ricardo and Gonzalo have the courage to take part in this workshop in systemic leadership together in Miami. The realisation: "Government can take away everything from us, our competitors can betray us". But what was healing to them was the feeling that "they can't take away from us what it means to be family". Deeply touched, the three of them connect to the source 'the sense of family'. Then, they connect to each other. Finally, they can look each other in the eyes without having to look away.

Example

Origin is also about roots. The móre people can and are allowed to be rooted, the more resilience they have and the less stressful events have an effect on them.

A few years ago, I facilitated? a constellation workshop for people at Social Services. It was for people in the so-called 'granite files', the people who had worked there for ages, people who were no longer fit for work and labelled 'ill'. Of the 21 participants, only three were physically ill. Amongst them, there were approximately ten different nationalities. During the day, something started to become clear to me: many of these people had come to the Netherlands as refugees. Some of these people had brought their own values about work to our country. They suddenly realised that if they wanted more of a chance in Holland, it could mean they had to be unfaithful to belonging in their country of origin. This realisation helped one of these people find a job within weeks. A year later, eight more had found a job.

What really became clear, was that for part of the group, people were cut off from their roots and origin. And the moment they were allowed

Jan Jacob Stam

to (re)connect to their roots again, they became strong and their talents could flow naturally. That strong in fact, that they may have become too strong for the civil servants at the social services and for Dutch society at large!

3.3.2 History

After origin, different events make up history. It won't be a surprise that we argue that leadership needs to have knowledge of striking events in the history of the organisation. Especially, because those events can be the cause of the workings the system getting stuck.

Perhaps important parts of the organisational system were carelessly lost. Think of important values, people, groups of employees, buildings, anything that is part or was part of the organisational system. If something has carelessly been lost, it is good cause for a system-conscience to bring it to light in a suitable way. Unconsciously, people can be stuck to things that are long gone form the system. Or better said: that seem to no longer be part of the system. Even employees that come into the organisation long after the specific event took place, can be 'employed' to bring something 'old' back into the picture. Mind you: the system conscience is often stronger than the person. The same wat dust can't help being sucked into a vacuum cleaner. The power of the suction of the system is too great.

Think of events like these:

- Departure of the founders and others in key positions
- Departure of groups of people
- New hires, functions, departments
- Change of vision and/or policy
- Farewell of products, brands or services
- Introduction of new products and services
- Other financial flows

- Moving
- Merges and acquisitions

3.3.3 Systemic ownership

It is usually pretty clear who are the economic and legal owners of a company. There can also be systemic owners. Systemic owners say something, in an unconscious way, about the course.

The systemic owners of a hundred-year-old gin distillery in The Netherlands, are the customers who drank their gin for an entire century and have thus become the ambassadors, due to their brand loyalty. The company was obliged to confer with them for their consent to making new drinks.

Example

The legal owner of KLM is Air France. The financial owners are the shareholders. The systemic owner are the Dutch people.

Example

One of the questions that we frequent is; isn't the characteristic signature of a founder, who gave his or her name to the organisation, for always the systemic owner of the organisation.

Was it even possible to begin with for the company Fokker to take a different course than the course that flowed through the veins of Anthony Fokker? They didn't try it, the whole Fokker system remained loyal to the philosophy and way of working of Anthony Fokker himself 'to the bitter end'. Could it, with the emerging future in sight, have been at all systemically possible to change drastically?

Our institute is named after the founder of systemic work, Bert Hellinger. Would it ever be possible for the Bert Hellinger Institute to stop working with the basic principles of Bert Hellinger…? We aren't going to try!

It is worth thinking about systemic ownership:

- *"Where as an organisation do we belong?"*
- *"Who's are we?"*
- *"If we are, or are becoming, a well-known brand, who is systemic owner of the brand?"*
- *"We made a start with crowdfunding, what does that mean for the systemic ownership?"*

Systemic leadership requires answering these kinds of questions. Systemic owners are important stakeholders of the organisation. They need to be consulted or be involved in significant changes or changes of direction. And it could be that a group of employees are loyal to different systemic owners. And it is useful information for leadership. Especially, if you come up against 'unexplainable' conflicts of loyalty with employees or a department. One of the implementing organisations of a Ministry that generates projects to make The Netherlands more sustainable, was struggling with the following issue: *"Do we belong to the Ministry of Economic Affairs, to private partners or to the end users, society?"*.

Once, an experienced entrepreneur came to one of our workshops on organisational constellations. Her question was why she couldn't manage to get her third brand marketed. The first two had been on the market for ages. And successfully so. She had invested a lot of time and money. Actually, everything had been ready to launch the third brand for a very long time. Still, it seemed as if something was stopping it.

When asked the question: *"Where did the money for this third brand come from?"*, the quarter dropped. Quietly, the answer was, *"From my husband"*. At the launch of the other brands, she had taken on the development together with her husband. This time, she hadn't even consulted him. This is where the unconscious entanglement lied: it needed his systemic consent.

3.3.4 Can you fúlly welcome your new colleagues?

People are parts of the whole. The whole called team, unit or organisation. Belonging requires leadership. It doesn't happen by itself. It means you have to make sure that everyone in your team is welcome with everything that they bring to it. You can't welcome someone without welcoming the background they bring with them. That background consists of many systems:

- earlier professions;
- education;
- family history;
- societal history;
- unprocessed periods or incidents, not just in the lives of your employees, but also their family backgrounds;
- religions;
- country of origin;
- ethnic background, etcetera.

Of course, you don't want all those backgrounds to become a (working) factor in the work place. But the good thing is: the more the backgrounds are allowed to be, the less it wants to play up and makes themselves be heard. Moreover, the more people are allowed to connect to their roots, the more violence and insecurity that are capable of dealing with.

Tell each other war stories. It is a good tool to make sure that the backgrounds belong in a connecting way.

3.3.5 Place and function

It is hard to manage a team is, as a team leader, you can't take your place in the organisation. A man who can't take his place as father, will find it hard to deal with problems associated with the upbringing of his youngest son. Here, too, order is important: first take your place, then you can act from that place. Acting without taking your place is often empty action. Much ado about nothing. 'Be' first then 'do'.

Functions for people or people for functions

In organisations, you need to take the difference between person and function into account. If a function doesn't have a place in the organisation, for example because there is a surplus of management, chances of success are nil. Even if the person takes up his function perfectly. The system in fact no longer accepts that the function exists, so someone can't be successful at it.

It happens a lot that functions in organisations are created and sustained without being necessary for the whole.

It could also be that the function in itself has the right to exist but that the predecessor keeps the place occupied, as it were. The predecessor hasn't, systemically, left yet. If the chair isn't vacant, it could express itself in the team working as if the predecessor is still there, which makes it hard for the successor to function.

Team of people

If you are a team of people, then it's the people who determine the character of the team. It's just like family. It also means that the possibilities and impossibilities of the team strongly determine what is and isn't possible. If there is no one in the team with sufficient IT capacities, IT related work has to be outsourced. And when someone leaves the team or a new arrival comes to the team, a new balance has to be found again.

Team of functions

If you are a team of functions, there is a big difference to the team of persons. Firstly, functions come to being from what is needed to reach the goals of the team. But the functions mainly offer continuity. First there are the functions and then you look for persons to fill the functions. In a way, it implies that the team system as a while precedes the (sum) of individuals. Continuity is ensured because it is clear which functions belong and which don't. The great advantage is that when someone leaves, the system is still intact. A new balance doesn't have to be sought. Of course, you do have to find a new person who can give the function form and colour.

Organisations often start as a system of people. As the organisation grows, it can be useful to switch to a system of functions. It is often a vulnerable period, the way a lobster is vulnerable as it molts. Moreover, often people who were worked hard to build the organisation during the first phase, don't like it when the organisation moves into a system of functions. Suddenly, they feel less welcome or seen as a human being. Obviously, being a system of functions doesn't mean that it isn't human.

In the organisation I work, we are moving towards self-organisation. Relationships are more equal and there is less need for hierarchy. People become more important than functions. Job descriptions make place for roles. — A.R.

Creating a function for a person

Creating a function for a person. If a person is valuable to the organisation and you want to keep them, you can create a function for them. But beware: this doesn't always work out well.

A consultancy wanted to attract a man who fit perfectly with the organisation. To bind him to the organisation, they created a commercial function which could possibly grow to be a great expansion for the company. The function didn't yet exist. Very soon, it became clear that the man in question was very welcome but that there wasn't any room in the company for the function. It was too early. — Example

---

The rule of thumb is that when you need a new function, you create the function first and give it a place in the organisation before recruiting. The apparent humane approach: *"you can shape the function yourself"* can cause many a systemic accident.

Employed without function

Keeping people employed without a function seems a humane thing to do, but it is actually not by any means. By keeping people and functions that are no longer necessary, excludes them. Horrible! This means, that as a systemic leader, as soon as you know someone doesn't have a place anymore, you must say so immediately. Knowing that you won't be extending someone's contract and not telling them until 6 months in is disgraceful. It takes away all dignity. And moreover, it is a good recipe to undermine the system and to rob the system of its power.

Other systems

Other than a system of people or a system of functions, we sometimes encounter other systems. For example, the system of brothers in arms in a successful Spanish organisation, founded at the end of the civil war. Profit is victory. Losing looks grotesque, gives cause for shame and loss of face. Opening a new market is a conquest.

Or a system of religions. Where I worked in the Dutch PTT-Telecommunication company, there was a subsystem of leaders that all belonged to a reformed church. Together, they called the shots in the company. If as a young manager, you aren't aware of this, you don't understand why your career isn't going as planned.

Family Business

The family system doesn't prevail in all family businesses. It occurs the other way around too: a company is legally and historically speaking nót a family business, but has the overriding characteristics of a family business. An advantage of a family business is that there is often a great deal of loyalty. As you know, there is no way to not belong to your family, starting from the moment you belonged. It is harder sometimes to find successors. Being a leader in a family business, when you are not part of the family, demands an enormous feeling of balance on the crosssection of what is or is not supposed to or allowed to belong.

Systemic division of property

When someone leaves, it is good to 'clean the seat'. This way, the potential of the available place as well as the potential of the colleague who

CHAPTER 3. NURTURING YOUR SYSTEMIC LEADERSHIP

left, remains. If the 'seat is clean', the newcomer taking up the function, will only have to fulfil this function and not have to deal with all sorts of systemic stuff that cling to it. Cleaning this up doesn't just happen. As a leader, you need to do something.

The more you acknowledge what was and what wasn't possible in the years past, the less will cling to the chair. It means that you need to let go of the motto: 'about the leaving employee, nothing but good'. This doesn't mean you have to put them down, on the contrary. What is important is to acknowledge what was and what wasn't possible. It is about acknowledging reality that purifies, not covering it with the mantel of love.

It is also important that the person leaving the company doesn't speak beyond the grave. It means there won't be able to claim anything back and forth.

It is an illusion to go your separate ways in complete balance of taking and giving. What applies here too, is facing the imbalance and refrain from being unhappy about it, demands a lot form the soul, ánd purifies.

Lastly, as a leader, don't forget to invite the colleague who is leaving to take with them their heart and soul or inspiration when they leave. People easily give their heart and sometimes forget to take them with them when they leave.

A good systemic division of property gives dignity and keeps the potential of growth of both systems high.

At every farewell, I speak the words of an employee who, after a period of more than thirty years in the same place, finally left and transferred to a completely different department: "Peter, we will miss you. As a person you are irreplaceable, this is why I want to thank you here today for everything you have contributed. That you took up L.B.

this place for so long and that you were connected to our team for such a long period of time. I thank you for what it cost you to make this contribution. It is now up to us how to continue and progress with your products, your contribution and your place. After today you will be gone. Peter, take your heart with you, take the source of energy from which you worked here with you. It belongs to you. So, take it with you. And everything that is unfinished between you and us, we will take. I wish you well in your new work environment."

A property settlement when you leave an organisation is painful yet helps bóth parties to be free and to move on. And don't forget to take your heart with you when you go!

New function or employee

A new function requires the right to exist, a clear contribution to the whole and clarity around the order in relation to all the existing functions.

CHAPTER 3. NURTURING YOUR SYSTEMIC LEADERSHIP   91

Once, we had a new function for Communications. Being the owners, we had an insufficient idea of what the function should contribute to the whole. Moreover, we weren't clear if in the order, the function should be next to or under the supervision of the office manager. You might get it already: enough ingredients for a lot of interference, confusion, and fertile grounds for insecurity of the person who was to take up this function. It was a good lesson! — *Jan Jacob Stam*

A new employee must be welcomed by the existing system in a fitting way. And in such a way that the employee knows that he or she belongs and where he or she can contribute and what their functional relationships are with other colleagues. As a rule of thumb, you could hold that the new function should be inaugurated by the two hierarchical layers above the incoming function.

3.3.6 Loyalties, conflicts of loyalty and Objections

People are loyalty-machines

If you are part if so many systems, with every change you may find yourself in a loyalty conflict. To whom or what will I be unfaithful if I go along with this change?

Taking a stronger place in one system can mean that you belong less to another system. It can make you hesitant to take up your place fully in the first system.

If I had been fully loyal to my family unit, I would nót have watched TV with my friends every Wednesday at the Catholic family Huizenga. But becáuse I wanted to belong to my friends, the consequence was that, in relation to my parents, I had to be a little disloyal. — *Jan Jacob Stam*

Often employees won't tell you when loyalty conflicts are affecting their behaviour or functioning. I someone is internally not at work but somewhere else, you might want to ask about it: *"Where are you with your attention?"* Please, don't make it sound like blame but let it be sincere interest. Thén it will probably become very manageable.

Objections

With every suggestion you, a colleague or other employee does in a meeting, you will find objections. In fact, it would be strange if there wouldn't be any. Objections are expressions of loyalty. That is the good news. Try to figure out from which system the objections are coming from? Yes, of course the objections are coming from colleague A. But which system is trying to speak through A? And on behalf of how many people does A speak? And what is the voice speaking through A trying to protect? Usually it is something that was valuable to the organisation or part of it. What applies here too: as a leader, the more you acknowledge that there was something valuable for the organisation, the less people feel that it needs to be protected.

3.3.7 Terrible things

Belonging has nothing to do with 'objectively' speaking either doing 'terrible things' or the right things. A suicide terrorist commits his deed to belong or be loyal to something. Probably the ultimate form of belonging.

This is the reason why as a leader you must postpone any judgment when an employee is being terribly difficult. As long as you have judgment around it, you can't see who or what the employee is loyal to by being difficult.

3.3.8 No and Yes

Development is only possible if you take the risk of no longer belonging to something. Saying yes to something new isn't very hard. But in every Yes, are many No's.

If you say *"Yes"* to something new, what are you saying *"No"* to or *"No longer"*? Often the problem doesn't lie in saying Yes to the new, but facing the consequence of the many No's and daring to speak out.

You must in a way be prepared to burn your bridges. And it is this preparedness, that taking of the risk, the remaining in the void, that is where the power of development lies.

You recognise this when you are following a course. Or your employees are. Often, someone has had extensive training and schooling in various expertise. To what extent is the new program more of the same or does it ask to be disloyal? Immediately, a program confronts, conscious and unconscious, loyalty conflicts with precious teachers and examples. It unconsciously, immediately creates the question: how much "*No*" is needed or are you prepared to speak out about how much "*Yes*" you can voice for the new program? And is it possible to develop yourself without saying "*no*" to something or something else?

3.4 Everything has a place (order)

Leadership ensures the order. In such a way that every person, each function, every team, every unit and every sector has a place in the order that you can count on. So nó energy has to go into the question: where are our anchors? Where do we fit in the order? What comes first, and what after that? Where do we fit in the production process?

Problems with order is a huge energy drainer. And that energy then can't be used for work, letting talent flow, for exchange in taking and receiving, for systemic turnover.

This is what makes order so important: it creates the conditions where lively workflow is possible. Without order, no flow.

In families, it is relatively easy to figure out where you 'belong' in the order. You date and time of birth 'determine' this. In organisations, there are more principles of order active at the same time. Seniority, like in families, is one of them, but it is definitely not the most important! With the basics covered in chapter 2, we will now take a next deepening step.

The different orders are, in order of importance:

1. Order in leading principles
2. Order in functions
3. Order in contribution to the whole
4. Order in seniority

In an organisation order often works counterproductive. That gives turmoil, tension, conflict, insecurity. By the way, it is impossible to find óne conclusive order. It is better to make all the orders visible and therefore manageable.

Summarising

- Systemic leadership ensures clarification of and order in leading principles
- Systemic leadership ensures order in functions
- Systemic leadership is aware of the function of middle management in an organisation
- Systemic leadership listens to the rebels of the organisation
- Systemic leadership acknowledges the difference in contributions to the whole
- Systemic leadership can intervene on tensions that arise from difference in seniority

3.4.1 Order in Leading principles

Leading principles of an organisation answer the question: *"As an organisation, what are we to the outside world?"*. Leading principles are about 'what' and not about 'how'.

Leading principles are in the DNA of the organisation. They are already there. That is a big difference with missions and visions, that are

CHAPTER 3. NURTURING YOUR SYSTEMIC LEADERSHIP

often made, built, constructed. Leading principles are the essential links between the organisation and the outside world. The products and services are 'merely' the carrier for the leading principles.

Leading principles have two sides. It is not only the answer to the question: what are wé to the outside world? But also: what does the outside world want us to be in the future?

The Leading principles of your team determine what your team is to the outside world and to other parts of the organisation. The Leading principles determine the identity of your team. And again: the products and services your team delivers, aren't the same as the leading principles. Usually, the products are the carriers of the leading principles.

- A windmill cooperation delivers electricity as a product to her members, but her leading principles are 'the feeling of giving more home to my home', and 'giving ownership of our raw materials'.

- A developer in Egypt builds houses, but offers 'the possibility to live safely'.

- Builder/entrepreneur in Moscow builds houses, but offers 'the bridge between communist and modern Russia'.

- A newcomer in the market of packaging delivers packages, but mainly delivers 'freedom for the receiver, with a rebellious wink'.

It is very useful as a team to know what your leading principles are. And to put them in an order. It matters, for example for a cultural centre in a city, if you have 'liveliness contributing to society' first, where 'offering culture' supports this, or that you 'offer culture' first after which 'contributing liveliness' comes second.

Every foundation for primary education in Amsterdam writes up a strategic paper, a plan for the future, an ambition. Whatever you want to call it, you could think. But language and the use of it is W.P.

a powerful systemic tool. The leading principles shine through the sentences, unconsciously there or trying to be present consciously. The order in leading principles shines through the sentences. The acknowledgement of reality, can be made explicit because change is on its way and it will possible require a sacrifice of some sort. You can feel it permeate through the sentences if there is a place for everyone in the organisation. Coming through the sentences…

When I was asked to write a directional plan myself and lead the process towards it, I tested as well as I could, in the sessions as well as with the people who were helping me out, if I complied with the systemic principles (the completeness of the system). I have become increasingly aware of how daily 'language-interventions' of leaders either strengthen or disrupt the systemic balance.

What if you are clear about what the leading principles are in your organisation. The next step is to find out which team members who are more or less are kin to those principles. Who is ambassador to which principle? And what is the systemic function of every team member here?

Keep in mind that every team member has its own leading principles: what is leading for him or her in life. If the leading principles are too far off or not reconcilable with the principles of the team, then there might be something to face. You can't escape it to sit down and talk to each other. That too, goes with systemic leadership.

Barbara Hoogenboom

We had a management team member a from Nature conservation and sustainable management organisation come to us one day. She was under the impression that the director of the organisation wasn't doing her work well and she had some strong opinions about it. My first tendency was to think of the pattern of parentification (chapter 4). A characteristic of this is that someone 'always knows better' than the boss.

In the constellation, something else became visible. It seemed that this person was more connected to the fight against poverty, than

CHAPTER 3. NURTURING YOUR SYSTEMIC LEADERSHIP

with protecting and preserving nature. I said: "So every euro that is spent on nature, is wasted money. Because it isn't being spent on a single mother who lives under the poverty threshold.?" "Ja" was the soft and powerful answer. The painful realisation followed that she was working for the wrong organisation.

If you know what the leading principles are of the whole that is called team, you know which functions are needed. Including their order. Leading principles constitute the most important force in the order of a team of an organisation. In general, there are two or three leading principles. There are rarely many more.

Leading principles are about the question what the systemic function of the organisation is. It connects the organisation to the outside world. 'if you consider life energy as a movement that wants to accomplish something in the outside world, then the leading principles are the effects of this life energy. With leading principles, it isn't about hów we do things internally but what we áre for the outside world.

What you can do with your team, is to try to find the leading principles. It often requires intensive questioning about: *"what are we to the outside world"*. It is about *"what we are"*, instead of *"how we do it"* or *"what we sell"*.

An important trait of leading principles is that they are already present in the core of the organisation. You don't have to come up with any or build any, as is the case with missions and visions. The advantage of leading principles is that, once determined, they are easy to communicate throughout the organisation. With everything you build, the law of thermodynamics teaches us, you have to give it energy to keep the construction standing. If you don't, it will fall apart naturally, as with everything you build. Constructed mission require a lot more energy to maintain than leading principles.

3.4.2 Order in functions

Leadership requires to take care of the order of functions in an organisational system. We zoomed in on the concepts Agency/ Autonomy and Communio/Well-Being in paragraph 3.1.

It may seem obvious to think: the function that comes in first place in the order, is management. But if you keep thinking in terms of boards, management, employees, you are thinking in organisational terms. We want to invite you to think in systemic terms, the systemic functions we have named above, are often carried out by management. But for a system this isn't really important. Even in self-directing teams these functions are necessary. And it doesn't matter who fulfils these functions. As long as they are. Every system needs them.

Those functions that create conditions to keep the whole organisation alive ánd give it a place in society, come first. To keep the organisation alive, for example, there needs to be money. It is necessary to have the right permits. This is the place where the identity of the organisation is determined. The position in relation to other players in the field or the market.

When you think of a school it is all about closing the financing. The choice for education, be it Montessori, Waldorf etcetera. About the design of the building.

The core functions of the organisation come in second place. The functions related to the first of the leading principles. Teachers in a school. The pharmacist in a pharmacy.

In third place are those functions that provide the necessary information so the core functions can carry out their work properly. The laboratory that needs to provide the necessary results to a doctor to be able to make the correct diagnosis. The amanuensis for the biology teacher. Without functioning microscopes, there won't be a biology lesson.

In fourth, we are moving into the direction of the communion-role. We make sure things inside the system are working smoothly. It could

CHAPTER 3. NURTURING YOUR SYSTEMIC LEADERSHIP

be human resources in a large book store. It could be the cleaning in the cafeteria. It could be the hostesses in a hospital. You can also distinguish these systemic functions within a team.

And these different systemic functions can also be found in óne person who works independently. Often there is a concern here for people who are considering starting a their business as a self-employed professional. All systemic functions are need, If as an artist you want to mainly make art, your core competency, you also need to manage sales ór make sure you find someone who can do it for you. What we often see with self-employed consultants, is that they love to live their core competency, but forget that they need to market it too.

The hidden role of middle management

There is a forgotten role of middle management. A role that requires exceptional strength and arm span.

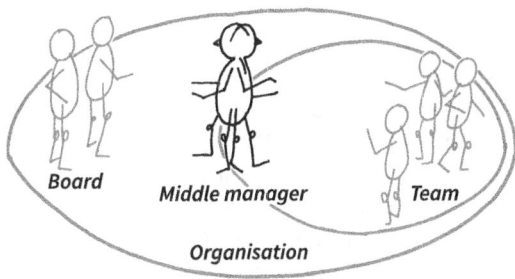

As middle manager, you are in the middle of unresolved issues in the larger system ánd the ones that suffer from this most is your team. This asks for a lot of leadership of you own position!

That role is the team leader one. A team is, without them knowing it, unconsciously, confronted with unresolved issues or opposite leading principles in the greater organisation or in society. The system conscience does that. Unconsciously.

As a leader, you are on the edge of the team-system. Your task is to keep unresolved issues from the outside at a distance. On the other hand, you must create conditions so that people inside the team can work well together.

Keeping unresolved issues from outside at a distance

Keeping the unresolved issues from outside at bay doesn't mean you should close your eyes to them. You need to look at them fully, sometimes even feel them. At the same time, you aren't in the position to solve them. It is not your job. And you don't have that kind of influence. Be mindful to not secretly try to resolve those issues, or to know better than your boss. Even if you do know better, trying to surpass your boss is disastrous.

If you say to your boss: *"I want you to resolve those contradicting leading principlesr"*, you place yourself above him or her. You have become his or her boss, you 'parentified'. Go ahead and try it, systemically, it won't work.

If you say to your boss: *"for my team to function well, I need this and that from your"*, you remain in your position. Even if your boss won't give you what you need, it is a far better starting position than being 'parentified'.

The next step is that you put your name to the task to see all these unresolved issues outside and acknowledge them. Without taking them on board. It means something to the extent of: *"I see all the unresolved issues outside. They are there! Not that I like them, but they are there. However, what I dó like is to create a good working environment for my team including all these unresolved issues"*. Then you turn to your team and say: *"In your work you are continuously confronted with unresolved issues form outside. Sometimes you are aware of them and sometimes they have a hold on you without you even realising it. I will try to notice it if you are suddenly taken by the impossibilities from outside. But please, also watch over each other. If someone is no longer comfortable it could possibly have to do with something in the outside world. And come to me please if you get stuck or are divided by something that is no longer possible because of something going on outside. Then we can look at it together and take next steps"*.

CHAPTER 3. NURTURING YOUR SYSTEMIC LEADERSHIP

Marjan is employer of 7 different general practice centers. Marjan: "Workload and pressures has increased enormously, while the minister (of Health) denies it. GP's don't feel seen, heard or taken seriously and it is at the expense of quality. There are increasing number of incidences. This goes against our norms and values. It is a nationwide proble".

The constellation shows that the original idea of the centers was to give GP's more freedom and now they are having to turn that back in. At least inside the centers.

When we set up a place in the constellation for the Minister and for three difficult files she has, it becomes clear that the minister doesn't have much freedom and is caught up, as it were, in Health Care issues. Once Marjan can acknowledge that, she doesn't have to be the 'long arm' of the GP centers.

When Marjan looks at 'her' GP centre, she can see that it is good to go back to the roots where it all started and to be grateful for the limited freedom there is.

Systemically speaking, Marjan has the function of middle manager: between the inside and the outside world. It asks for the ability to separate and connect at the same time. It asks to not fall into the trap of going into an impossible battle from a parentified, nor to be defeatist.

"Have fun in lingering in the field of unresolved issues instead of enduring them. Enduring is surviving, lingering is living."

Jan Jacob Stam

A rebel is someone who breaks away from the order. Usually upwards. There are two common responses to rebels: the first one is to set the rebel straight, 'pushing him or her back into place'. The second one is to evict the rebel from the family or family unit. From a family or organisations point of view, rebels are annoying: they disrupt the peace, they ask difficult questions and often it feels as if they are sawing at your legs. Parents and managers often experience the rebels' behaviour as a personal attack. This is really a misunderstanding. We have never met a rebel who rebels with selfish reasons.

The rebel

The rebel breaks away from the order because he or she has important information about the system as a whole.

A rebel truly knows and feels that he is taking a risk of being ousted. There must be something more important than the risk of being evicted. What strikes you when you zoom out, is that rebels often have information about systems as a whole. Rebels are prepared to make their own needs secondary to what the system as a whole need.

Because rebellion often points at the layer above, it feels to managers as if it is personally targeted at them. We can both remember how it felt in the days when we had management positions, when someone was nipping at our heels.

However, a manager, other than the person he or she is and other than the function he or she has, also representative of the greater system. Where would manager find the courage to really listen to the message the rebels have about the entire system, instead of putting them in their place or sending them away from the organisation?

JAN JACOB STAM AND BARBARA HOOGENBOOM

CHAPTER 3. NURTURING YOUR SYSTEMIC LEADERSHIP

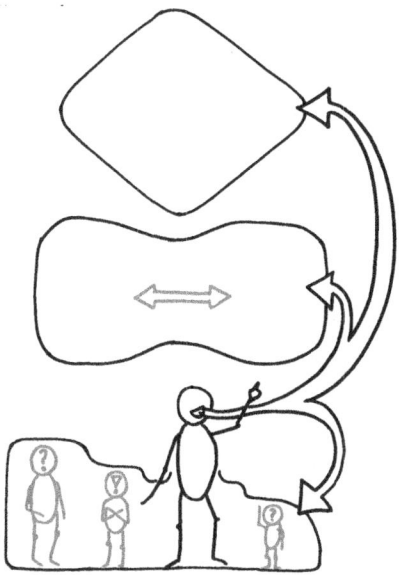

The rebel wants to touch upon belonging or exchange. He or she is often not 'understood' because he or she is literally 'out of order'.

If we repress rebels or evict them from the system, we lose the information that they have about the whole. How worth our while would it be to listen to what that important information that the rebel is conveying, even if it's formulated in a crooked way, before we take measures against the rebel? This means of course that if you take the information seriously, something may have to change. And that is not always going to be nice.

3.4.3 Contribution to the whole

Contributions can be about the past, the present or the future. It is about contributing to the survival of the system as a whole. A contribution means that you or someone else, or an entire department, has delivered something. A system wants that delivery to be compensated for, that you receive or take something in return. It has to be in proportion. More important than being compensated, is the acknowledgement of the contribution. If you compensate someone without acknowledging their contribution that compensation quickly feels as if you are being bought.

Past

Think about all those people who have made a contribution to the organisation as it is today. You won't have missed the fact that, also painful periods and events contributed. And because of that, they may be acknowledged.

Example	*A Polish entrepreneur who felt stuck, was brought to tears when he expressed: "Without the communist period, we wouldn't be who we are today as an organisation".*

Acknowledging difficult periods often means to act 'politically incorrect'. Founders have of course made an important contribution. The same way people have opened new markets. And inventors of new products. But also, those who were there befóre, who made it possible for the organisation to be born.

Present

Think about those people making an important contribution to the continued existence of the organisation. Which functions, which people. Even if they don't display it. It can be acknowledging, connecting and supportive of flow when organisations acknowledge and celebrate contributions, aside from compensation for it.

> **Bert Hellinger is the example of modesty. But let's be honest: without the Second World War, the young rebel Hellinger would not have grown into who he did. And he wouldn't have had all these systemic insights that are the foundation for this book.**

3.4.4 Seniority

- How old is each person in the team?
- How long has each person worked in their current job?

CHAPTER 3. NURTURING YOUR SYSTEMIC LEADERSHIP

- How many years has each person worked for this organisation?
- How long as each person worked for this team?

Acknowledging seniority is important to uphold the growth potential. Giving older employees the chance to reorient themselves on the last working years of their lives, can contribute to the overall feeling in the organisation: 'this is a good place to get old'.

It can also be uneasy. Younger employees are sometimes faster in their field than older employees. A healthy team requires acknowledgement of both. If young, capable employees unconsciously feel: *"It is weird to deliver more and better quality than our older employees"*, then you must beware that it doesn't stop the flow.

Almost by definition, the next generation must have the chance to contribute ore and different than the previous. That is the essence or growth and development. It is the task of leadership to acknowledge and balance the different aspects of seniority.

Tool: making seniority visible
- However simple this tool may seem, it is always an exciting process to do with your team:
- With your team, stand or sit in order of age. Clockwise, starting with the oldest. If you do this in a circle, you can see each other and it gives you more information than when you stand in a line.
- How does everyone feel, now that you are in order of age? What is good and what is awful?
- Also, look at the entire team: does it look good and logical? Is the whole balanced and calm or does it look strange and with holes?
- Then, sit in the order of the amount of time you have been in this field of work or years of working experience.
- What is better and what is worse for every team member (the parts?) and how is it for the whole? Ask people about what they see.

- Another beautiful one that acknowledges the past, is to stand in order of how long you have been in this particular team. And ask the oldest: what did you find when you first started in this team? Did you have processors? What did the organisation look like at the time? And ask everyone similar questions. Maybe memories will surface of team members who still belong somewhere in the order of the start and who are no longer here. You could even give these colleagues an empty chair.
- OR try this one: how much do you contribute to the whole. Or if there are many different functions in the team, which functions go in which order.

3.5 Honesty in taking and giving (exchange)

What leadership needs to do here, is to take care of exchange. And in the right dose. And at least on two fronts.

3.5.1 Between the mutual parts

Life wants to produce. That goes for people but also for organisations. Life apparently wants something with us. One of those things is to let our talents flow. To a right degree. And in the right direction. So, our talents can actually achieve something. Preferably in the outside world. It is also called achievement or result.

Every human being has talents, attention, dedication, muscles and time to offer. Talents want to flow. If you see talent as something that flows through someone than something that comes out of someone, then you can see every person as a source.

Leadership needs to take in to account that employees' talents can achieve something. The way an arrow can hit the rose. An energy leak can have the consequence that talents can't achieve their destination anymore. People work hard, people give it their best, but it all seems to be leading nowhere. That is exhausting. Not the effort but the fact that the effort leads to nowhere.

CHAPTER 3. NURTURING YOUR SYSTEMIC LEADERSHIP

For satisfaction to come form effort means that the effort has to lead to something tangible or palpable. Satisfaction is a form of gratefulness. Of course, there are forms of satisfaction: *"Look we are better than the competition!"* As long as that satisfaction gives the competition to grow too, even outside their own system and direct sphere of influence. If satisfaction means that others in the same branch can also get better, the satisfaction doesn't only contribute to the development of the organisation but also to the development of society. Satisfaction is gratefulness. And it is gratefulness that makes us happy. Not dreams or plans.

In the field of Energy Transition, we found that satisfaction meant: proving your own right: taking out the competition; feeling better than the competition. This kind of satisfaction is actually triumph. It excludes other.

Example

If talents can't flow, they dry up. If someone is payed too little for their work, there is dissatisfaction about the exchange, it is imbalanced. To get back into a healthy balance someone must give less of their talents. The flow becomes thinner. Logical, but a shame. You should have a systemic audit with your employees from time to time about if talents can flow freely. Should talents be more directed or less appreciated? Direction and size of te flow, that is what it is all about.

Vice versa: if you pay people too much for their achievements, what happens? It starts with an employee who increasingly feels as a non-adult. A child. This asks for some explanation. A child is given life from his or her parents. That is só much, you can never give that back, with whatever talent you have. You can only pass it on. This is how the flow of life and generations come to being.

If someone is being paid more than he can achieve he will, unconsciously, see the organisation or leader as a parent. He gets more than he gives. This is how he ends up in a parent-child position. The employee stops growing and developing as a self-conscious employee but as a dependent child (which may give loyal and obedient employees, but is this what a system needs?).

Eventually, if the employee can't compensate for the money he gets, it becomes unbearable for the soul. And can't be fed to the self-worth anymore. The employee is forced to break the relationship. So, if you want to lose someone, pay them too much!

3.5.2 Exchange between the organisation and the outside world

Another task of systemic leadership is to monitor the flow between the organisation and the outside world. Which products and services can reach society and do something useful?

Sensing and having the wisdom to know which products have potential is a systemic leadership talent.

The potential of a product in itself isn't enough. Society must be able to hook up to that potential. You need to know the suitable channels to let the potential flow. Without this talent, a system can't survive.

Frustration is blocked life-energy

If there is frustration in an organisation than that is good news: life energy! Systemic leadership need to recognise and acknowledge it. Then it is all about pulling the plug so that the life-energy can flow again.

Jan Jacob Stam

Writing this book, gives me more energy than certain other projects that just don't seem to be flowing. This doesn't mean that by writing this book, other 'stuck' projects don't get any more attention. On the contrary. Part of the energy that is generated by writing this book, I can use for more strained projects. Writing to me, and my surprise, is a process of taking.

3.5.3 Funding

Government funding is the same as paying an employee too much. How much funding do you give someone or an organisation to remain in an independent position? A child-position.

CHAPTER 3. NURTURING YOUR SYSTEMIC LEADERSHIP

Funding is systemically un-free. Also, the norms and political colour of the funds comes with the money. When the funding is such a large amount that it brings you in a position of dependency, the funded organisation is doubly burdened.

We saw this happening with artists: when the government funding was abolished, some of them became more powerful.

In a collective of artists that was advocating to reinstate the Dutch Caribbean islands in a museum in The Hague, our political capitol, we saw that the government funding and all the unresolved issues of the Ministry of the Interior and Kingdom Relations of The Netherlands, came on the shoulders of the artists. Some of them literally broke.

Example

Placing solar panels rocketed when funding was stopped.

Example

I can remember this well. The first solar panels that we placed on our roof were given with government funding. Yes, I unconsciously used the word 'were given', even though I paid for them. But as a compensation I had to have an energy performance measurement taken. I didn't feel entirely free and independent with those first panels. I was grateful that I could buy them. After the government funding was abolished, we bought multiple panels. At our own cost. That felt free! And it raised my sense of ownership and autonomy. Funding took away some of that.

Jan Jacob Stam

When, as a systemic leader, you read the previous paragraphs, you may want to think about which costs you make and which part you want your employees to take, for their schooling and development. I can't give you easy arithmetic or an easy answer. But you may be able to use this as a guide:

- Which amount makes the employee and his achievements stronger, which amount weaker?
- Which amount connects more and which amounts makes him or her freer?
- Which amount leads to more free flow, what stops the flow?

We deliberately use the word 'free flow', because achieving from a space of guilt about an amount being too big is not free flow. It is more doing repentance.

3.5.4 Money

Money in itself is nothing. It is always about what the money means. in our systemic practice, we have never encountered that a company's only goal was profit. Profit always had to dó something. Protect, stroke an ego, give position, guarantee existence, take fear away etcetera.

A suitable amount of profit is a sign of a healthy system. Loss can also be a sign of a health system. Too much profit or profit at the expense of people's health eventually has an effect on the system as a whole.

Money is complicated. If you want to research the meaning of money, profit as well as loss, you must be precise. Money is often viewed through the lens of judgment, prejudice and preconceptions. Money is of course virtual. Most of the money circulating doesn't even exist. But we count on it to convert it into goods. Apparently, we have all been compromised to a certain system with patterns. Even though we might openly strive for a more equal distribution, or more 'honesty' and 'justice' (systemically speaking there is no such thing as the absolute worth of justice), something allows the monetary system to be as it is. Something allows the enormous division in a lot and very little money. We co-create this system. We judge ánd co-create it. And íf we would want to change something fundamental, it starts with acknowledging that there is something deep inside of us that is worth so much that we keep this system alive.

Money as the colour of the money-giver. With funding, inheritance and investments it turns out that the source of money, its values and maybe even the leading principles of it, comes along with the money received. Keep that in mind when accepting money.

Lastly, people have a very precise feeling for the amount of money that is fitting as compensation for a service performed.

With the following steps, you can stimulate this sense for balance:

- Does this reward (funding, benefit, investment) makes us stronger or weaker?
- Do we achieve with a higher or a lower quality?
- In the end, are we freer or more bound to the giver of the money?
- Can we, after the transaction, look each other in the eyes freely?
- Does it contribute to more gratefulness?
- Does it make us lighter or heavier?

Vary with different sums of money, then you will quickly find the correct amount.

3.5.5 Influence and Power

Influence is power that flows. That is why we discuss influence with the principle of exchange in taking and giving.

Power, the ability to get something done., belongs to a certain position in an organisation or societal system. As a manager, your function gives you the mandate to do certain things in an organisation. In any case, your part of the organisation must meet the objectives set. Meeting your goals means producing and achieving a lot of systemic turnover. You need influence for that.

It is tricky with the amount of influence you use. If you exert too much power, more than is suitable for your function or place, or with more violence than is needed to get it done, it could be that you are seen as authoritarian and lose your authority.

Jan Jacob Stam

As a teacher, leader of the class, my punishments in class were sometimes tóó strict. I had the short pleasure of a class that did what I (really) wanted them to do, but that obedience was always short lived. I lost the respect of the class.

If someone is authoritarian, it is immediately clear to everyone.

The other way around is sometimes even more harmful, when you take less influence than fits your position.

Firstly, the energy leaks, people become groggy, start doing other things than the priorities you gad set. But it could also be that more and more people start waiting for you to take decisions that go with your position. If it takes too long, informal leaders will take a place next to or above you. In short: if someone keeps using less influence than suits his or her position or job, the system slowly collapses. Moreover, the order is no longer clear. Formally yes, but systemically more of the principles of order start working against each other.

Patterns

4

A 'pattern' is what we call the phenomenon that people, - in a family, organisation or other group- repeatedly take up the same position or the relationships between the members of the group keep following the same – often unwritten – 'rules'.

4.1 Patterns, Habits and Procedures

A pattern is different to a habit or a procedure.

- A habit is ingrained behaviour. Because it is ingrained, it is automatic and increasingly unconscious: actions as we drive, brush our teeth with one hand on your back etcetera.

- Many processes in organisations are captured in procedures: clear steps in a work process. These are often written down, agreed upon and everyone is aware of them. You can consciously deviate from a procedure when a specific situation asks for it.

What we mean in this book with a pattern, is: unconsciously end up in a same sort of place in a system and acting from that point.

The relationships in a pattern interact with each other: if part of a team finds themselves in a perpetrator position, the other part of the team 'automatically' goes into the position of the 'victim'. A person, a group, an organisation or even an entire country, can show behaviour that stems from the system conscience. Be drawn into a place without knowing or wanting it. That is why it is unconscious. Pattern emerge aside from free will. If someone would say: *"You have put yourself above your boss"*, that wouldn't be correct. It implies that it was a conscious choice of the person involved. And it is not. There is probably someone or something missing in the system, drawing the person in the vacuum above the boss.

4.2 How patterns form

Patterns arise because of the survival mechanism of the system as a whole (the system conscience). This conscience ensures that the system can continue as an entirety, if necessary at the expense of individuals. Patterns are the systems' reactions when one of the workings of the system are constrained, often because someone or something is being excluded, because of an unpaid debt, because the order was disrupted.

Patterns are solutions, reactions of a system. Irrespective if it's nice. The difficult thing with the system conscience and thus with patterns, is that they work unconsciously. Without knowing or wanting it, you are drawn into a system and, as it were, 'employed for the greater good'.

You can view families, organisations and society as a constellation of patterns. And those patterns made society, organisations, the family you grew up in and you, to who you have become today. Patterns exist independent of persons. Individuals come and go, are born and die, but patterns can continue. Patterns can go on for hundreds of years.

Because we have worked in so many different countries, we have come to recognise, identify dominant patterns per country or region. And those patterns almost always form as a response to events in a country: the flow of migration, colonialism, domination and the countries' location. For instance, The Netherlands lies between the Anglo-Saxon and the Gallo-Roman part of Europe. A dominant pattern in Mexico in a way is a Calimero-pattern: *"They are big and we are small. Poor us"*. A dominant pattern in Australia is: *"Everything is different than promised"*. Not better or worse, just different. This started in England with the convicts who thought they could go back to England after they had served their time in Australia. And this applied to the soldiers guarding them too!

4.3 The function of patterns

Patterns ensure continuity

A pattern ensures that a system can continue existing. So even though it can be tough on the persons who 'are employed' by the pattern, it is vital for the survival of the system as a whole. This is of such vital importance that the basic patterns can continue on and 'pass on to' new colleagues if some of the old colleagues leave. This puts forward an important question for those organisations that say goodbye to an entire group of employees at once because of 'innovations'. How long will it take before the new employees are 'employed' for the existing pattern...?

Patterns ensure stability

Patterns keep the system, be it an organisation or a society, together. It is the glue between individuals. In a matriarchal society for example, there is a pattern where the women, mothers, 'official' or not, keep families, companies and societies together.

Patterns ensure predictability

In unstable situations, in a future that is unsure, patterns offer guidance, to know what position you have in a system and thus to know where you stand.

These 'positive' functions of patterns also have an unwanted side. When the world around us changes, an organisation needs different patterns. You can suffer severely from patterns that you keep falling right back into. Whole teams for that matter. Often, patterns are useful and helpful for a while. Until patterns start becoming a little tight because for instance, the family company wants to become a multinational due to a crisis. Then, patterns become obstacles.

CHAPTER 4. PATTERNS

4.4 Patterns attract patterns

Similar patterns have the tendency to attract each other. Systemic leadership wonders: "Do we need more of the same or different patterns?"

A well-known pattern is, unconsciously, wanting to fulfil someone else's task or responsibility or even their burden. If this is the patter you live in, you will be easily attracted to work situations that are familiar with or need the same pattern.

Everyone hiring new people will unconsciously tend to hire those people who are in the same pattern as they are, or have the same pattern that can also be found in the organisation. As soon as you are aware of the mechanism "*Do we need more of the same to reach our goals or do we need other patterns?*". You could think of a diversity policy: and then: diversity in patterns.

That patterns attract each other, happens at work as well as in private situations. Often partners either have the same pattern as their loved one or complementary patterns. A team that had issues around feeling unsafe, calls to a pattern of 'colouring inside the lines' as well as the complementary pattern of reckless behaviour. It isn't good or bad, it just is. Its repercussions can be different though. A pattern in a private situation could be a blessing and a curse in a work situation. And vice versa: a pattern that in a work situation leads to a better career and success, could be weighing you down privately. This is why, when we describe patterns, we try to distinguish the impact for both the private and the work situation. Patterns occur with individuals, within a team, inside as well an organisation as a whole but also in the relationship between the organisation and society. Lastly, entire provinces, countries and nations often have repetitive patterns.

Example

In the province of Groningen for example, there is an overriding pattern of polarity between 'city' (the city of Groningen) and 'surroundings' (Groningen's countryside). For centuries, they have held about an even amount of power. The city is dependent on the production of grains, sugar and other agricultural products to remain a centre of trade. Vice versa, the countryside is dependent on the city for infrastructure and coordination. And so, they keep each other hostage. Both, the city as well as the Countryside were able to grow like this for centuries. Who ever wanted to venture into something in Groningen had to understand this mechanism.

The province of Friesland has a different pattern. Traditionally, there have always been 31 noble families spread over the province and ruling from their castles and the eleven cities. They keep each other balanced, neither of these units could be allowed to become too powerful. This pattern, too, was good to know about if you wanted to venture into something new in Friesland.

And these patterns repeat themselves within smaller units. A farmer whose gigantic farm was situated against the 'Groninger' sea wall, was considered master at his company (City). He always spoke of his employees as 'my workers' (Countryside). These workers had small housing on the farmers' land.

We often see that patterns in society spread to organisations as a whole. This often happens during the founding of the company. There is a logic to that. Many organisations are founded because something is going on in society that requires an answer. That is why organisations tend to develop a pattern that in essence, in their origin, is either the

CHAPTER 4. PATTERNS

same ór complementary to the pattern in society. A pattern like that can stay around for a very long time, even if society had changed enormously. And that society asks for different patterns.

4.5 Getting rid of patterns

Once you are aware of the obstructing pattern in your team or organisation, you will want to get rid of it. To want to rid yourself of patterns is actually a good recipe to have them repeat themselves. The system conscience won't be thrown off that easily. If you want to get rid of a pattern, the system will no longer be complete. It will 'try' with all it's might to let the pattern remain, even if it means by detour or through the back door.

There are four intervention-direction to deal with patterns:

1. Become aware of it
2. Untangle it
3. Grow beyond it
4. Disrupt it

4.5.1 Becoming aware of the pattern

Patterns that you are aware of, are more easily managed. But you aren't aware of most patterns. You just live them. Our observations so far is that by becoming aware of them, they are more manageable but that doesn't make them go away.

In paragraph 3.3.2 you read about becoming aware of a pattern in the section on the Ministry of Economic Affairs. About how the oil crisis in 1973 started the pattern 'unity for everything'. This pattern has been around for half a century. But now we are aware of it.

Acknowledging the pattern reduces the effect of the pattern

There are two ways to recognize and acknowledge a pattern. The first one is by acknowledging that the pattern has made us who we are today. Without the pattern, the 'unity of everything', the Ministry of Economic Affairs wouldn't have become who they are today, nor could they have performed as well. Expressing genuine gratitude together for what it has brought us so far. Reap together how the pattern has helped historically, has protected and has helped grow. Thése are the recipes to help reduce the workings of the pattern.

Storytelling and laughing about how you were caught in the pattern as an entire team, is liberating too.

The second way is to acknowledge what caused the pattern to start. In the example of Economic Affairs: the Yom Kippur war in the Middle East. Mind you, President at the time, Jimmy Carter, used to find it so hard to fight the oil crisis that he called the crisis: 'The moral equivalent of war'. In a war, 'Unity for everything' makes sense.

4.5.2 Untangling

Untangling patterns means becoming aware. Not only of the pattern that is keeping you trapped, but also how it is tied up with the patterns of your team or organisation.

Let's say you have a pattern where you are easily inclined to mediate between two opposites in conflicts. In jargon: triangulation. It could be, for instance, that, with your pattern, you are regularly invited to board level because that is where (unconsciously) the opposites that make the flow stagnant are. Firstly, this causes a pattern on the demand-side: the board where something can't come together. Secondly, is the pattern on the supply side: you or your team, that feel comfortable in situations where there is tension.

By untangling patterns, you start to see where patterns attract each other, or are sometimes not compatible You untangle entire knots of patterns which causes your team feel more freedom and freedom of choice to deal with the patterns.

In this example, the awareness of the demand ánd supply side. On the demand side, you may not be able to change anything, but on the

CHAPTER 4. PATTERNS

supply side you now have choice because you have become aware of the pattern.

Other than untangling these patterns in different parts of the organisation, it may also be useful to untangle patterns in different situations or contexts. Triangulation, for instance, has very different benefits and in a private situation works differently than it does in a work situation. It could be very powerful to know what works in one context and what doesn't in another context. This is also a form of untangling, but more about the untangling of different contexts within which a person finds himself.

The pattern of 'Other people's (life)task' causes me to be overworked in my job, but in my sport, where I don't give up quickly, it helps me do well in the competition.

Jan Jacob Stam

As a mediator, I led many a conversation between managers and employees in an organisation working for a better environment. What struck me, is that both manager and employee were very fierce in these conversations. Even though emotions are part of these kinds of conversations, the fierceness of what I encountered was of a different order. Especially about the manager, I would be surprised every time.

I realised that I was at the table with activists. Fighting runs through their veins, is their mission. I you aren't prepared to fight, you are a bad activist. The pattern of fighting was necessary to be able to do your job well, to do what needs to be done. The relationship with the outside world, that which you are fighting against, is of lesser importance.

Later, I discovered, the best activists are the ones who climb the hierarchical ladder quickly, and I realised what I was meeting at the table: the relationship is of lesser importance than the conviction that (being) right is on your side.

Barbara Hoogenboom

> *Becoming aware and untangling this pattern, makes it possible to choose (again) if you want to continue this pattern with your internal relationships with your colleagues and employees.*

4.5.3 Growing beyond

Growing beyond a pattern is like growing out of your childhood clothes. You grow past your youth by taking it entirely al part of you. You grow beyond a pattern, by taking the pattern, including the good and the bad, completely. The way to leave your youth behind you is by incorporating it completely in who you are today. As an unbreakable part of your body, heart and soul. Only then, after some time, will the pattern stay behind, while you, your organisation, can continue to grow into the future.

Once you grow beyond, you can't return: you can only give up your youth ónce. That is a high price to pay, so sometimes it is wise not to say *"Yes, I want that"*, too easily. From a systemic perspective, your youth will never return after you gave it up.

In organisational terms, the origin of an organisation is its youth. The more you take accept? the origin of the organisation, the less the organisation has of repetitive patterns that, as it were, hold it in the past.

Example

Henk was the fifth-generation owner of a construction company. He came to us with a question about succession. Henk has two sons. Both work in the company. Henk wasn't sure which of his two sons should be his successor in the company. Henk's insecurity, otherwise so deciding, was surprising. When we discussed the history of the company, a traumatic event from the war came up. Because of this event, not the eldest son but Henk, the youngest, took over the company.

It was a rebellious act of the young Henk, in an attempt so safeguard the company. Because Henk was the better candidate for succession, he 'disrupted' the order between the brothers. Of Henk's two sons, the

CHAPTER 4. PATTERNS

youngest was also the better candidate. But Henk, systemically sensitive as he is, was feeling very restless about it. The sentence: 'War is part of our company for good', caused Henk to commit the war, the disturbance in the order, then into his heart. He could grow beyond. After this, Henk was much calmer about the succession and in the end, made a suitable choice.

4.5.4 Disrupting

Crisis and war are mechanisms that can destabilise só strongly that it causes room for new patterns. It is the work of the evolutionary force that can destabilise those patterns.

A way to disrupt patterns, without the entire system to fall apart, is controlled chaos.

A home-care organisation was in a deep financial crisis a few years ago. Part of management asked us for help with a constellation. The only thing the constellation showed was how hopeless the situation was. The managers gave each other that look: "So this is truly the case". In a second constellation, we set up a care provider and a user. The position of the care provider in relation to the heath care user requires working meticulously. The position is as such that the user holds a lot of autonomy over the demand for care, over the budget and especially over their own life. The care giver is in a position where he meets the user as an equal, and not as a replacing 'parent' or 'servant' to the care giver. The managers are on the edge of their seats and were watching, fascinated. One of them said: "This is the core of the relationship between supply and demand that we can build an entire organisation around". Because of the urgent situation, there was a willingness to let go of existing patterns and let the disruptive workings of the crisis do its job and give a new pattern a chance.   *Example*

4.6 Common Patterns

There are dozens of patterns in organisations. To get an idea of how you can think and feel in terms of patterns, we will discuss a few common patterns, without trying to be complete.

The way we have described patterns, is a little more mechanical than in reality. The systemic reality can't be described in cause and effect; systemic reality multi-layered. With more complex connectivity than the sum of many cause-effect loops.

Common patterns we will clarify here:

1. Ending up at your managers level
2. Ending up above you managers level
3. Taking on someone else's tasks
4. Carry out a task because of an unconscious promise
5. Seeing more than what or who there is
6. Connected to what is no longer here
7. Colliding extremes
8. It will go south if we do it and it will go south if we don't
9. Success prevented!

4.6.1 Ending up at your managers level

In jargon: triangulation

Triangulation is the pattern where someone ends up on the next higher level.

With triangulation, you get drawn into the next higher level. Tempting and at the same time also awkward.

Triangulation that you see often in organisations, is a team coordinator who enters the space of his managers Management Team, a secretary who stands next to the member of the board, and an administrative officer who is the right hand to a project manager and has become a fixed worth to the project meeting with the client. Triangulation is also possible for entire departments. The 'support staff' as often described by Mintzberg, the supporting departments like HR, are often triangulated. Entire organisations can be triangulated. Think of paying agencies that have become triangulated between government and beneficiaries. NGO's are often triangulated: they fill a place where something that doesn't work in the relationship between government and citizen.

Entire countries can be triangulated. The Netherlands, because of it's position between the Anglo-Saxon and the Gallo-Roman part of Europe. The Netherlands has, for example, made trade, the bridge between the two cultural major powers, her religion. Another example is Finland, traditionally in a special position between Sweden and Russia.

Triangulation is a pattern of temptation. You get drawn into something where you don't naturally belong. A lot of advertising appeals to triangulation. There is a Dutch ad, that appeals to the 'Security of the Swiss life', meaning to be comfortable after your pension. The ad makes you feel 'at home' in a situation that is not accessible to everyone.

Triangulation is the pattern of the bonds. Winking is often triangulation. *"Join the club."* Especially when not everyone is allowed to see it, that wink.

"As team manager, I became friends with a member of my team. We shared a passion for walking. Unnoticed, we spoke about management issues during our lunch walks. People started noticing our lunch walks and soon people started talking about us as a couple. Even though I was able to refute this, this form of triangulation wasn't right. Unfortunately, it meant that we couldn't go on our lunch walks anymore."

How triangulation in an organisation starts

Triangulation is a common pattern because at certain levels in organisations something is missing. Something necessary to be able to function well or to be a unit, is missing. If, for example, at management level, there isn't enough strategic insight, chances are a department or person will be invited to a management meeting. In the natural order, staff comes after management. If a staff department is called in for strategic advice, and systemically speaking becomes part of the management team, this is a disruption of the natural order.

Another common phenomenon, that there are unspoken differences in a management team and for instance, a senior consultant or favourite team leader is invited as a decoy. The role of this distraction isn't called as such, it looks as if subject specific expertise is being called in. In the meantime, it is all about mediation, to help change a way of thinking, to clarify, to build bridges, to smooth the way.

How triangulation in a person starts

The origin of this pattern lies in the family system. In a family, triangulation starts when two parents can't form the system 'parenthood' to-

CHAPTER 4. PATTERNS

gether. If love between the parents can't flow. When the male love can't reach the woman and the female love can't reach the male, for whatever reason, the child is drawn into the relationship of the parents. The child gets triangulated. This isn't the fault of the child, nor a conscious choice. The power of the system to draw the child in is too strong. The system-conscience 'wants' the man and woman to be a unit(y) because it is good for the continued existence of the family line. If the man and woman can't form a streamlined unity, the child is 'used' to that end.

There are always good reasons why a man and a woman fail to be a unit, even if they form such a 'good match' to the outside world. It could be that the man is strongly tied to his family, or to fallen comrades in war. A man is then physically but not emotionally with his family unit. Or when a woman is still very connected to her mother, for instance because the mother died during childbirth, then she is physically but not emotionally available for her husband and children. A different example is that one of the two is unconsciously strongly connected to earlier or another loved one.

Children can also be drawn into the upcoming divorce if their parents, by separating the parents unconsciously to stop arguments or unconsciously wanting to get the parents together again. They literally come between the parents, at the level of the parents.

Mother's-sons

When a son gets drawn into the family system, he becomes a so-called mother's son. A mother's son more or less takes up the place of the father. This often causes tension or rivalry between the father and (mother's) son.

The unconscious message of the mother's son to the mother, is: *"I will do anything for you. I will make sure you have everything you need"*. The mother's son's mission in life is: saving women, ánd al that is equal to women, like saving the earth, or groups or organizations. A mother's son who grows up amidst triangulation, develops many talents. Sensitivity for one. And they know what women need. They move easily in groups. Mother's sons are often great consultants and coaches.

Mother's sons are often good mediators, especially in those cases where the clients' job in his family of origin was to keep the parents separate or to bring them together. Professionally, these talents can be very useful. Patterns aren't just difficult, they also create enormous a lot of potential useful qualities.

Father's daughters

Father's daughters are drawn some more into to the position of the mother. They fulfil that which can't flow freely from the mother's side. There is often tension with the mother. A father's daughter is Daddy's little girl. She is sensitive and knows what the father needs. Translated to organisations: what leadership needs… In their work, father's daughters know how to deal with authority. At least they are not afraid of it. Because they are comfortable moving at the layer 'above them', father's daughters easily make a career. Sometimes it doesn't require much effort at all and they are invited in. Patterns attract patterns. Father's daughters are easily distrusted by colleagues as again and again they are invited for sparring with the boss or the management team. Usually, the father's daughters are blamed and not the management team (the father).

Barbara Hoogenboom

When I worked as a team leader of a financial institution, we were acquired and taken over by a larger bank. After the acquisition, my manager, who was loved and kept the group together, had to leave out the back.

Other managers came, from inside the organisation, competing banks as well as form the acquiring organisation. At one point, I was invited to take part in the weekly management team meeting at the layer of my new manager. I was flattered, it made my job even more interesting and I tried my best to contribute value where I could.

In retrospect, with the knowledge of organisational systems today, I realise that my contribution was mainly in the relational sphere of influence, as a decoy, and a bridge builder. Banking, I realised, was something the, mainly male, board members were quite capable of themselves.

CHAPTER 4. PATTERNS

It also worked against me. After all, you hear information that isn't meant for you. Others, like my colleague team manager, and my team members, know I participated in these meetings. It required some maneuvering to stay loyal to the Management team, my own layer and my employees. Undoubtedly, my colleagues will have viewed me with some suspicion.

Glass ceiling

There is an important footnote for father's daughters. The pattern is a sécret pattern. Mother, who knows full well that her husband misses something, unconsciously agrees that her daughter replaces her. But never openly. The pattern is almost a hidden contract between mother, father and daughter. If it becomes too public, the daughter retreats. Therefore, you sometimes see father's daughters make a career quickly and as soon as they are presented as CEO, they suddenly feel an inner retreating movement: the systemic contribution to the glass ceiling. How can a father's daughter grow beyond this pattern? By making peace with mother and everything that comes from mother's side. In systemic terms: taking the mother ánd her background fully.

Midlife crisis

From a systemic perspective, the midlife crisis is the process where people – especially triangulated- embrace the parent (-side) that up until then, couldn't be done before. For a mother's son, this means to stand in his masculine energy fully, shoulder to shoulder with the father. It also means saying *"no"* to the mother: *"I won't do everything for you anymore".*

This process is often accompanied by a change in jobs. Changing jobs isn't as much an attempt to break away from old patterns. It's much more that when a father's daughter embraces everything that comes through the mother, she gets access to many new qualities. To be able to love these qualities, she has to find a goal. Something in the outside world. And to let these qualities reach their destination, you choose a job that is fitting.

Recognising the pattern of triangulation

People that are familiar with the pattern of triangulation:

- Are more backstage than in the spotlight, it is OK for them to be in the shadow.
- They usually don't make much noise, they won't be the first to voice their opinion.
- Are drawn into situations at the next-higher level where they really don't have any business.
- Are drawn into conflicts as a mediator.
- Easily understand opinions from different perspectives.
- Are often confided in about secret or sensitive information
- Often feel the appeal to build bridges, to mediate, to create understanding between different parties.
- Can have jealous colleagues because it comes easy to them to mingle with higher layers in the organisation.

Teams or organisations who recognise this pattern, can asks themselves this:

- Are we, as a team, easily drawn into tensions in the organisation?
- What is our systemic function? Do we sometimes fulfil a role in a relationship between parties or stakeholders who can't reach each other?
- To whom do we say: for you, I would do anything?

Making use of triangulation

With every pattern, you can ask yourself how you can use it for the good at work? Here are a few suggestions:

- You can use triangulated people well in situations where there are many different stakes, where people need to listen and where sensitivity is needed.

- You can use triangulated people well in supporting roles with project managers, managers, at the 'second' position.

- You can have triangulated people work with people higher in rank: they aren't easily impressed and are mostly open ánd cooperative. Triangulated people often feel comfortable in situations where there is care needed for the whole.

A triangulated position doesn't work as well in situations where someone (the triangulated person) is responsible for the bigger decisions. It definitely doesn't work when there are multiple opinions and a decision needs to be made by the triangulated person him or herself.

When I worked as a sales manager, I was manager to both the back office as well as the sales representatives. I am very familiar with the pattern of triangulation well. I was good at building bridges between the two teams. That was necessary because the two can moan about each other. We were a good team, it was fun, there was respect, good communication and good results. But when decisions needed to be made when there were contradicting ideas, I needed back up and consent from my manager. Not because he wanted it, but because I didn't dare carry the responsibility by myself.

Barbara Hoogenboom

Interventions with triangulation

If you can tell that your team is triangulated, and you want it changed, there are a few things leadership can do. Firstly, to be aware of the pattern, to acknowledge it.

Then, you can dive into history and ask yourself what this pattern once was a solution to. Where is the gap in the system that was filled by your team or organisation? Who brought you to life? With what intent? What did it produce? And what did it cost?

If you want to break loose from this pattern, it means taking your place as a team. To no longer solve somewhere else what needs to be solved. Leaving the responsibility there where it belongs. Taking the risk that elsewhere it may go wrong and focus on your true task.

Example

A group of HR employees of a hospital is at their wits end. They have to tell their staff that, under the cloak of job rotation, they aren't functioning well enough and will be transferred to a different department. The HR employees feel that this task is placing them between management and the employees. They feel that it isn't right and it weakens the entire system. Insight into this triangulation already gives some sigh of relief.

To stop the triangulation, they tell their management: "We have done this job with professionalism and involvement for a very long time. But it is not our task to tell employees, in name of management, that they aren't doing their jobs. It takes all power away from leadership in this hospital. We have decided to step out of the middle between managers and employees."

4.6.2 Ending up above you managers level

In jargon: Parentification

With parentification, you are drawn abóve your managers. A good place that gives room for your opinions. But it is also a place that eventually will weaken the entire system.

CHAPTER 4. PATTERNS

With parentification you end up abóve the next higher level.

In an organisation, parentification means that someone systemically, inwardly, places themselves above his boss. So, you aren't literally promoted as manager of your boss, but systemically you are in that place. You think, act, speak and feel coming from that position.

It counts here too: entire organisations can be parentified. Or is it parentified? Knowing better than someone else. Knowing what is good for someone else, something you often see with consultants, doctors or teachers. Also, those who represent other people's interests, can be parentified, think of patient or traveller's organisations.

Parentification is a disruption of the natural order and can lead to a lot of unrest.

Where once, the Dutch government, immediately preceding a war said to its citizens: "Please go to sleep, your government will watch over you", we now see a deep Dutch pattern of parentification. In fact, it is the whole concept of a makeable society a form of parentification. — *Example*

Entire departments can be drawn into this pattern. Specialists often know more about a subject matter than their managers, but in the hierarchical order they are below. It is logical that sometimes, specialists feel better than their boss. In earlier times, this was solved by the master – companion model: make sure the boss is superior on the subject than the employees. Departments, such as techno-staff, as described by Mintzberg, can easily be parentified. They have to come up with things that are 'good for others'.

As teachers in an experimental secondary school, we were parentified in many different ways. Pupils in class were divided into so-called — *Jan Jacob Stam table-groups, as diverse as possible. An image of an ideal society. Deep in our hearts, we felt the better parents to the students. School was an extension of the families at home. We also felt superior than all the other schools in the city. Actually, we felt superior than the entire society. This secondary school no longer exists and has merged into standard education.*

A.R.   *At the staff bureau where I was a manager, there were different professionals; educators, quality assurance, research and internationalisation consultants. In an environment where things change quickly and in an organisation with a lot of ambition, his managers in the primary process (education and research) were a little insecure about their actions. Our consultants quickly got caught up in a dynamic where they wanted to solve things for management. Consequently, the manager wasn't showing any responsibility for the solution. This struggle is the subject for a conversation between one of the consultants and myself.*

I start noticing the same dynamic in me. It strikes me that I am strongly leaning forward across the table and I want to solve it for the consultant. I tell him what I am experiencing. The pattern between the manager and consultant is now also between me and the consultant. After I named it, it creates room and we don't need many more words. A few days later, I hear that the consultant is satisfied about a conversation between him and his manager for the first time. The manager showed a sense of responsibility after which the consultant could remain in his own position.

How parentification in an organisation starts

The cause of parentification is that something is missing in the next layer above. There is a gap in the system. There isn't enough ability for decision making. The board of the foundation isn't doing what a board should be doing which causes the director, as it were, to rise above the board. It is a very nice position for freedom of action, but ultimately, it will collapse the cohesion in the system. In fact, if this happens in the

CHAPTER 4. PATTERNS

highest regions hierarchically, you can assume it is happening throughout the organisation.

Often the argument for parentification is 'weak leadership'. But it pays off to zoom out and wonder why leadership isn't being fully taken in this organisation.

As mediator in labour disputes, I did many mediations for the same middle sized national organisation. Usually, it was a meditation between a member of staff and his or her manager. I always met a parentified employee with a lot of judgment around the manager. The employees had often filed written complaints about the manager. A few times it even reached the board. Also, usually, an employee of HR was involved in the mediation and with that there was the confidentiality obligation. This way, after many cases, I was able to ask: "in general, how is trust in leadership in this organisation?". The answer: "Oh, nobody trusts his or her manager. And the executive board doesn't trust the supervisory board either…"

Barbara Hoogenboom

This organisations job was to organise elderly care. The health care sector is very 'suitable' for parentification.

Hoe parentification starts with persons

The origins of this pattern are, as almost always, in the family system. In a family unit, this means that someone becomes the parents of their parents. You are concerned with or have an opinion about your parents as sf you are their mother or father.

If parents' parents (or one of them) is unavailable, then that causes a gap in the system. That gap wants to be filled by the system-conscience, the grandchild is drawn in. The grandchild, inwardly, takes up the place of the missing grandparent for the parent.

The child can start feeling responsible for the parent: take care of them, listen to the – also information that isn't meant for children-. Sacrificing themselves, their childhood gets less of a chance.

Parentification, like other patterns, is a deed of blind love. Blind, because it happens unconsciously. The tragedy of this blind love is that it can never succeed.

The other side of this pattern, is that it goes hand in hand with many judgements about the other. Feeling better than the other. Indeed, you are doing something that your grandparents couldn't do themselves.

Ideals and parentification

Ideals can be a good recipe to get parentification. Sometimes ideals ask for a better society, a better organisation. If this means: *"better than others"*, parentification is lying in wait. Some ideals require improving the flaws of previous generations. The Hippie generation of the sixties wanted to improve the faults of the generation that 'caused' the Second World War. This whole generation is parentified.

Recognising the pattern parentification

People who are familiar with the pattern of parentification:

- Often have an outspoken opinion of management. Management stinks, should be doing other things, etcetera. Expressions of parentification focus on the wrong area. Management is just the symptom for what is missing or unclear óne layer abóve them.

- Are comfortable giving their opinion. They dare to take risks and are prepared to sacrifice themselves for a good cause. They dare to be lonely. It is a functional pattern for certain types of entrepreneurs.

- Often feel better or larger than their manager. You can often see it physically. They can literally blow themselves up, shoulders back, chest forward, chin up, arrogant look.

- As a child they sometimes ended up in the position of the parents of their parent.

CHAPTER 4. PATTERNS

- They inwardly feel bigger that the person or group that they feel pity for, or that they want to help, while it isn't a logical position.
- They end up in a position 'too high' for them in the organisation, a position they may not be able to handle.

Teams or organisations that recognise this pattern, could ask themselves:

- In which situations do we act arrogantly?
- As a team, do we often have opinions or judgments that make us feel better than the people we have opinions about?
- Who or what are we looking down on?
- Which important information do parentified groups in the organisation have about the system as a whole? How can that information be used for the greater good of the organisations. What counts for this pattern too, is that awareness is step one.
- Acknowledging that we are rebels and we use our worth? Read paragraph 3.4.2 again if you like.

Making use of parentification

- You can use parentification people in your organisation for tasks where they need to judge situations, where persuasion is needed, where people need to be directed to a new situation.
- You can use parentification people in your organisation to strengthen the autonomy of a project or where something needs a boundary.
- Parentification can lead to creativity and innovation: *"We must be able to improve this!"*.
- Parentification also means knowing 'what is good for you'. Coming from this pattern, it can make great sales representatives.

Think of all the departments that are parentified and how it helps to reach their goals.

A parentified position works less with the following:

- Integration
- Letting others find their own autonomy
- Negotiations
- Care

Parentification takes growth potential and maybe even dignity away from people or groups over whom you are parentified.

Interventions with parentification

If you can tell that your team is parentified, and you want it changed, there are a few things leadership can do. Firstly, to be aware of the pattern, to acknowledge it. Then, you can dive into history and ask yourself what this pattern once was a solution to. Where is the gap in the system that was filled by your team or organisation? Who brought you to life? With what intent? What did it produce? And what did it cost?

A parentified position also gives status and influence. Even if the status isn't official. If you want to rid yourself of this pattern, it mainly means letting go. Letting go of the battle you were fighting. Letting go of status. Stop fighting for certain groups in society or against certain forces in the organisation or society.

Acknowledge that the want to fight for or good cause or against something, is a deed of blind love. It is important to acknowledge that love and dedication and to harvest that. There is the risk that when you let go of the entire pattern of parentification, you also let go of the love that is locked up in it. That would be a shame. Untangle the dedication, the love that worked as a motor to become parentified, from the inappropriate position that you found yourself in. When you give up the position, you can focus your love and dedication on to something else. The love stays available, the position doesn't.

If, as a middle manager, you find yourself parentified because the higher management isn't doing what is necessary, the recipe is to stop

CHAPTER 4. PATTERNS

the fight first. That is not always easy. It also means you have to tell your team: 'I feel where things are lacking for you, I am not in a position to force that, I will no longer (with my full consent) be used to do so'.

You also need to let management know or feel that you will give up the fight. It means you no longer meet management from an inner place of feeling above them, but beneath them. And from that position, you can say: *"We need something from you. To be able to do our jobs well, we need..."*

4.6.3 Taking on someone else's tasks

A person or a team often does the tasks or carries the responsibility of someone else.

Sometimes, without realising it, we take on someone else's tasks. It makes us tough and strong, but watch out for a burn-out.

The pattern 'taking on someone else's task' is an unconscious pattern. A person or even an entire department can be 'employed' to fulfil someone else's task or carry someone else's responsibility. This is often triggered by the thought or the feeling that the other isn't strong enough to do it themselves. *"I will do it for you, then it is lighter for you"*, the pattern seems to say in you. And sometimes it is even stronger. *"I will carry the debt for your deeds"*.

As a manager or colleague, it is good to recognise this pattern. It can be quite an unobtrusive pattern and it is tempting nót to want to see it! Tempting, because this pattern creates people and departments that work hard, are extremely responsible and make sure the job is done. Great, right?

But there is a catch to it. This pattern is one of the best recipes for burn-out.

How the pattern 'Taking on someone else's task' starts

People who are employed by this pattern, are unconsciously connected to one or more persons in their family of origin who wasn't capable to fulfil their task and/or couldn't 'do what had to be done'.

This could be as direct as the parents, but usually, it stems from previous generations of grandparents and great grandparents. And we can't always trace back who it is about, simply because people often don't know their exact family history. It can also be that someone is connected to more than one person in the family tree or even with entire communities or groups. Someone who is familiar with the pattern and is conscious of it, often has a sense and 'knows' this is about someone specific or no which side of the family this pattern could have started.

Unconsciously, offspring, tries to do what couldn't be done. And it translates to the present and to do-do-do, take work from someone, be responsible for what's not yours etcetera. If you are taking over other people's tasks, you never know when you are done. Your body just stops one day.

Example	*You could ask yourself why The Dutch people gave so much money after the tsunami in South East Asia. As if it was more up to the Dutch than anyone else in the International community to help those affected. Which account had to be settled? What, unconsciously, did we want to compensate for?*

Recognising this pattern

Just give someone you know a load of work. If you can see the arms reach out even before he or she has had time to think about it, chances are he or she is very familiar with this pattern. Or when you ask someone who has obviously passed the age of 50 or 60: *"How many more years of work?"*. If the answer is: *"Well, I never really think about it. Definitely passed seventy or eighty..."* the pattern is probably familiar to them.

People or teams who are familiar with the pattern 'taking on someone else's tasks'

- easily tire or show signs of burn-out.
- are quick to help when a task presents itself and no one else is willing to do it.
- quickly say: I will do it or we will do it.
- often feel like a barrel that doesn't fill.
- can physically have developed a tough body (think of marathon runners) or have a large body that can stand a lot of heat.
- could be burdened with a high rate of absenteeism.
- easily fill the strained places in an organisation, on positions where others wouldn't risk it or where many people have been turned off by them.
- sometimes feel they must repent.
- can be classified as a true workaholic.
- Love work that requires stamina: endurance athletes. Don't send them on a sprint.
- They see what needs to be done; they often set a high bar, too high.
- Under the surface they are sometimes angry. That is logical because they are often prepared to take on a project that is too large or too heavy. On the one hand, they take tasks that are too heavy or too many assignments at once, on the other hand they complain about it.

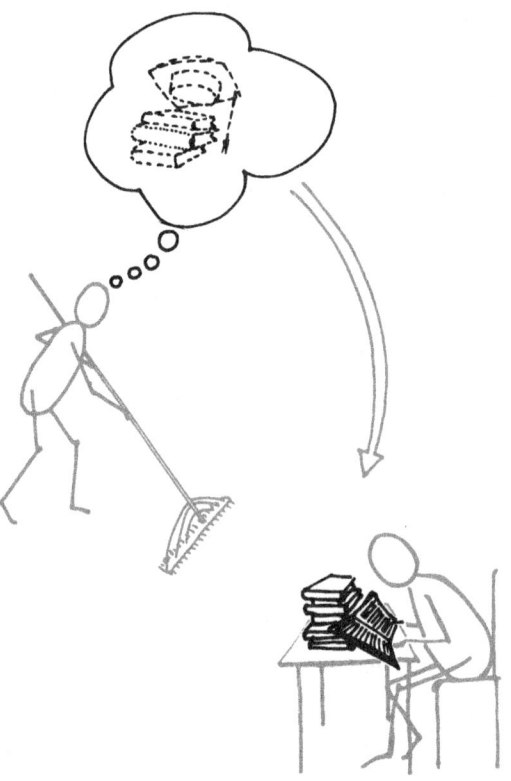

Unconsciously finishing the study someone else couldn't do. It provides drive and at one stage, the question: "for whom am I doing this?" "What do I want?"

Interventions for 'taking on someone else's tasks'

Firstly, and probably most importantly is, to be aware of this pattern in your team or with your colleagues. Talk about it. If your colleague recognises it, you can start making agreements about boundaries and who guards those borders.

What you can also do, is give your colleague a stack of work (paper) and ask him or her what part of this burden belongs to someone else. Intuitively, your colleague will know. The next step is to, symbolically, ask your colleague to lay down that part that of what he or she carries for someone else, there where it belongs. If that 'feel right', even if it is

CHAPTER 4. PATTERNS

hard to let go of, there must be way for your colleague to do that in his or her daily work.

Pattern-talks could be a good component of a performance review.

Preventively, a lot could be won in organisations in The Netherlands, if we can recognise burn-out at an earlier stage and prevent it. Reality is often the Dutch Calvinist nature and a work ethic that is characterised by "*it is to your credit that you work yourself to a standstill*". This isn't a work-climate in which you will see the shadow side of this pattern – and impending burn-out- early on.

Entire departments are sometimes captured by this pattern. It would be good for a department to at least ask yourself once in a while, whose task it is you are trying to fulfil.

4.6.4 Carry out a task because of an unconscious promise

Once, unconsciously, in a split second, a promise was made. "If it were up to me, not another child will ever be bullied". That promise determined my career.

It is often more painful to see others suffer than to suffer yourself. Sometimes, we see someone else suffer and, unconsciously, in the moment, we make a promise that will influence our life enormously.

A girl sees other children being teased at school and she decides: *"If it is up to me, that will happen to no one ever again"*. The promise goes underground. But she ends up going to the pedagogical academy, becomes a teacher and a good one at that.

During a tour through the slums, the Brazilian Fernanda sees the half-eaten nails of children because the rats have been chewing on them. She decides; *"No child will ever go through this if it is up to me"*. She becomes president of the state bank who also has a social obligation to the poor. Later, she goes on to build millions of houses for the poor people of Venezuela.

The promise has you instead of you having the promise. Often, this promise is a motor to pursue and accomplish a lot in life. These kinds of promises occur much more often than you would think. Ask yourself, or ask some entrepreneurs.

Sometimes, however, a promise becomes restrictive. Not becomes there is something wrong with the promise, but because life wants something different from you. Life has a different destination for you than what you are doing today. And then the promise becomes an obstacle. And a reason to dwell on it.

Recognising this pattern

The symptoms of this pattern are very similar to the symptoms that are zo typical of 'taking on someone else's tasks'.

Questions you could ask someone are:

- With who or what in your background do you feel connected when you do this work?
- On behalf of whom or what are you working this hard?
- Who wasn't lucky enough to have someone like you around?
- What can never happen again?

CHAPTER 4. PATTERNS

- Has it always been your mission to do this work, or was there a specific cause?

Entire departments and organisations can be unconsciously based on a promise. For example, the Alpes d'Huzes, 'Giving up is not an option'. The organisation makes the conscious promise "*Nobody will die of cancer again*", and we suspect the founders also made unconscious promises that made them strong motors behind this organisation.

I once did a constellation for the Rijkswaterstaat (Dutch Infrastructure Management), which was about teams who are responsible for the storm surge barriers. Even though it is more than 65 years ago, employees today are unconsciously driven by the promise "no man will ever drown again because of a flood". Also, all employees who were born after 1953 and employees who don't have any roots in the province of Zeeland. This promise is deeply rooted in the organisational unit.

Barbara Hoogenboom

Interventions for 'unconscious promise'

You can ask yourself if these kinds of promises are realistic. Most promises are, if you take them literally, a good example of a mission impossible. And unconsciously, the person or the tea, feel that mission impossible. That is what makes it extra hard to work at, that's what makes that the promise can become overwhelming.

It may start with realising on behalf of who or what or after which event you made this promise. Making the unconscious promise véry explicit, reminiscing about every little detail. And when it concerns an entire team, that everyone shares their memories with everyone else.

The second step is to harvest what it brought you. How it made you who you are today, how it influenced you, what skills it taught you. What return there was, who were able to enjoy that and profit from it. How it served society.

The third step, is to make an inventory of what the price was of the unconscious promise. What was not possible. Who else was burdened in a way because you made this promise. Make conscious where the problem lies today and why it is too much to ask to fulfil the promise for a full 100%.

The fourth step is a step where it will help you if you use your imagination. That you bring the people you once unconsciously made the promise to, into your imagination. That you look them in the eye and inwardly tell them how hard and with how much dedication and love you worked for them to fulfil the promise. With everything it gave to you and everything it cost you. That in the future you might allow yourself to change this commitment. And that it may keep you connected in a different way than was the case up until today.

Who knows, in your imagination you may see a smile on one of their faces, if you allow yourself...

4.6.5 Seeing something different than is there

In jargon: Double Image or Context Overlapping

Double image: I look at my boss, but I feel and act as if my father is in front of me

CHAPTER 4. PATTERNS

Double image is the phenomenon that we project on to a product, person. Country, religion and yes, on a leader, without being aware of it.

An employee speaks to you, but behaves as if you are his father. You see a well-known brand or logo and you immediately associate it with an adventurous day with your friends.

An employee wanted to talk to me about the fact that everything he tried didn't seem to work out. Fear of failure was used as an argument, but why wasn't really clear. After we set up his goal in a constellation (on the ground), I let him set up the obstacle to that goal. It was directly in front of the goal. When I asked him where his parents were in the constellation, his father was right next to the obstacle. The confrontation was huge. The dominant father had always been kept small in his own family heritage and could never 'harvest' what his brothers and sister did.

The question alone whose life the employee was leading, gave him the insight e needed. Today, he has taken new steps.

L.B.

We constantly project. Often that is not a bad thing but sometimes it gets in the way. When in a performance review, you want to let your employee know that it is all right to make mistakes and you motivate him edge to leave his comfort zone more often, it can happen that your employee says yes but doesn't act on it. Not from ill will, but because he and you both can't see the work environment is actually a film being replayed about the family of heritage of the employee.

One day, a lawyer of a middle-sized firm came to me with the question why she was finding it difficult to take a step towards either receiving a fair share of the turnover or to leave the firm. She felt great hesitation to sit down with the owners, a man and a woman, and openly discuss how she was feeling and about working together. Deep in her heart, she felt her time at the firm was up and she should

Barbara Hoogenboom

be spreading her wings. She felt small in the face of these two people. Which in itself was strange, she also admitted, because she was a big girl and very confident.

During the constellation, the (representative of) the lawyer looked at the representatives of the founders in such a way that implied something else. Whenever she looked at the founders, she was also unconsciously looking at her parents. Suddenly, she understood why she was feeling small and suddenly she understood why it was so hard for her to have that conversation. Suddenly, she understood the insecurities that leaving the firm would entail. The step would be synonym to leaving the family home!

This example isn't an isolated case: often the organisation is the so-called substitute for home. A company has something and gives something to the employee, that in their own family unit today or family heritage can't be found or was missing. Systems want to be complete.

Double image is very normal. We live in so many different systems, that it is logical for one system to be projected on to another. For reference: horses in the wild live on average in 1.8 different systems. During the course of our lives, we are part of fifty or sixty different systems. No wonder, context shifts from one to the other!

To be absolutely clear: double image isn't good or bad. Sometimes they strengthen a situation, sometimes the constrict.

Recognising this pattern

As a leader, you should recognise double image. It is a strong source of conflict between people, without being able to put your finger on what the real reason for the conflict is.

Someone who suffers from double image:

- responds in a specific way to a specific person differently than he would normally do in the same situation.

CHAPTER 4. PATTERNS

- can suddenly starts to falter opposite someone he or she would normally not do that.

Interventions for double image

If you are under the impression that someone suffers from double image with you or someone else, you could ask them:

- what if you have an extreme aversion for a certain behaviour, who or what does that remind you of? What film is this a copy of?
- If you look at that colleague, do you see that person or more the project goal or his task?
- If you look at your colleague, what else do you see? Does your response to him have more to do with the colleague or with that 'what else'?

The basis of an intervention for double image has three steps. You don't have to take all three, sometimes one or two is enough.

The first step is to find out what else that person, other than the person who the double image is projected on, is seeing. By pulling the overlapping films apart you are able to put them next to each other.

For example: *"When you look at your manager, you unconsciously also see the risky project he is trying to implement"*. If that is right, then this could be sign of double image.

After that, you could ask the person to imagine that they are two separate entities, the manager is óne and the risky project is the other. It might even help to make it visible with cups or something different to visually put them next to each other.

The second step is 'systemic parking'. Realising that the reaction to the other person has a lot to do with a reaction to the risky project. Maybe you could express your opinion about the project in a different way and no longer have it come between the working relationship.

Step 3 is to examine which other positions the two colleagues could take in relation to each other, after separating the films and the systemic parking. Maybe it becomes possible again to work together in a new way.

Double image with objects

Double image doesn't only occur with people but also with objects.

Jan Jacob Stam

A project leaders question for an organisational constellation: "In the Netherlands there is an increased tendency to pave gardens. All these paved surfaces together have a negative effect on water storage (overloaded sewers), but mainly on global warming. What can we do to motivate citizens to refurbish their gardens?".

This example illustrates double image when it comes to thriving gardens. A garden is much more than a garden. A garden has a certain significance to the owner. And that significance is projected on to the garden. Amongst citizens who pave their gardens, there is a group who see their garden as an expression of their entrepreneurship, taking matters into their own hands.

For another group paving citizens who are unaware of the effects of the set-up of their garden on water storage and warming, the garden is a possibility not to have to look any further into the world. A place where you aren't constantly confronted with all sorts of stuff and misery in the world. A trusted and pleasing safe haven.

Now it becomes interesting. The project leader doesn't have any power to enforce any behaviour amongst citizens. His move can only rely on information, conviction, temptation, threatening etcetera. But if you don't know or realise what a garden is other than a piece of ground, paved or not with plants, vegetables and a gate, it becomes difficult to reach the garden owners. Systemically speaking, it is necessary to work through a detour of the double image. When an owner of a garden sees his garden, he sees the meaning of the garden. More so than a collection of plants, stones, woodwork, furniture and ground. If you want to tempt people to change the set-up of their garden, it is important not to want to change the significance of the

CHAPTER 4. PATTERNS

> *garden. You could even use the significance of the garden as a leverage! So, with the entrepreneurial citizen, you could address his or her entrepreneurship to make the paved garden permeable.*

In a large Dutch organisation, who scores highly on sustainability, their sustainability projects appear to be giving meaning to the work of the employees. Their work becomes richer and more useful. But it seems more or less coincidental that it is about sustainability. It could also have been about refugee aid, as long as it makes the, sometimes boring, work richer.

Labels

Systemic leadership requires a phenomenological look on things (see paragraph 2.5). Every name and every label you slap on something, makes it hard to keep an open mind and look at things. Systemic leadership asks of you to not give any labels. Every label that you give takes something away from the potential of the person behind the label.

> *In a certain disadvantaged region of the Netherlands you can find many a beautiful initiative in Health Care. A consultant in elderly Health Care, who comes to us with a question, has observed that some of the citizens who réally need help, aren't being reached by the initiatives. Soon it becomes clear that when you label people as 'someone who réally needs care', you inadvertently create a double image You can't really see the person, women, child for who they really are anymore.*

Jan Jacob Stam

4.6.6 Connected to what is no longer here

In Jargon: identifications

Identification is the pattern where someone or an entire team is unconsciously loyal to someone or something who was excluded or threatens to become excluded.

In the real world of humans and organisations, people are often excluded, closed off, dismissed, etcetera because we want or múst continue. We break the contract with the manager who didn't perform well enough and continue with the order of the day. This policy has served us for years, but now that it o linger suits us, it is replaced by better policy. From an organisational perspective, this is perfectly logical and good.

But the system-conscience will inevitably start 'interfering' with it. The system as a whole 'agrees' that respectfully, everyone should belong, good or bad, old or new, needed or outdated. It is not that as a leader you can't make any changes, it's about not having people carelessly on unknowingly having people or values leave through the back door.

So, identification is the pattern where someone or an entire team is unconsciously loyal to something or someone, who is being excluded or soon to be excluded. What if an employee has committed fraud and was fired on the spot. No one speaks about what happened with the other employees. Then it could be that years later, employees start identifying with the fired person or a same kind of fraud is committed.

We named it earlier, a general rule you may recognise: you become what you try to avoid. The more you try not to resemble your father, the more you find out over the years, that you do…

At an organisational level this applies too: whatever you fight, will come back to you via a detour. What isn't allowed to be, will come back in through the back door.

Identifications are a reaction of the system to the exclusion of people, values, identities or other important elements that have made a family, organisation or country to what they have become today. The system-conscience isn't talking about right or wrong. If, as an organisation, you can't or won't face the fraud, it's a good recipe to have the fraud continue in distorted ways.

How identification starts

Identifications start out of pure good will. This is important to realise. For example: *"We must change now. The world outside won't come to any standstill. If we don't change now, we will miss the boat."* It is logical to want to leave the past behind when there is a sense of urgency. That happens on the basis of the unit conscience: we want to and must belong to the future. We can't dwell over the past and belong to the past. And in the rush, it is forgotten to acknowledge al; that was once important, to acknowledge. That is when the system-conscience intervenes.

Another cause for the rise of identification is protection or shielding.

In a government department, there is a culture of fear. This department is merging with the same departments of two other municipalities to one new organisation. The frontman of course wants to build an open atmosphere. "We will forget the culture of fear of department Y. Let us please talk about more positive things. There is so much good work to do." Logical! But that isn't how it works. Employees feel: "Things have happened we can't ignore and pass. We don't feel acknowledged and seen. It tears us apart, there is a lot of absenteeism".

Example

Keeping employees out of the wind is well intended, but has the opposite effect.

Resistance to change

Resistance when the old is cast away, affects employees who are connected. Often unconsciously. A form of identification with that which was lost or is at risk of being lost.

Resistance to change, who doesn't encounter this in his or her leadership? With systemic change of thinking, you find out that resistance to change often has to do with loyalty to someone or something. Loyalty to something that is at a risk of being lost. An important value, a way of working, a person, a group pf people, an identity of a team or an organisation. If you are up against resistance in a team. You can immediately ask yourself this: *"who or what are people connected to? Who or what can't disappear?"*. If you look at people who show signs of resistance in this way, you are instantly connected to the larger system. Resistance is a good indication for the pattern of identification.

M.L.

He was recalcitrant, separated himself from the others, was often away and said "no" to almost everything. More than demonstrably, he would be conspicuous by his absence at meetings or was late. He said "no" to almost everything and always sat arms crossed. People just let him be and said nothing. That is just the way he is they said.

At first it really irritated me. It felt as if he undermined my "authority". It felt as if he didn't accept me and excluded me. What was I to do? When I confronted him with his behaviour, I would see a smile. As if he enjoyed it. As if I had accepted an invitation and he seemed to enjoy the fact that I confronted him. It felt as if I was drawn into the invitation but also into a pattern. I had to snap out of it to be able to take a

CHAPTER 4. PATTERNS

bird's eye view. I started reading up in the history of the organisation and found out that he was the last member of a now no longer existing team. All other team members form this team had long left the organisation, most took their pension but some had been a forced departure.

I couldn't change the situation. I could, however, acknowledge what he was doing, namely keeping the old team standing. And with it, keep it alive. I decided to talk to him about it and to let him know that his hard work for acknowledgement had not gone unnoticed. That gave room, room between us to take next steps.

He isn't quite there yet, meaning, inwardly he still remains in that space a little bit. This is because acknowledgement for this team had to come from hierarchically higher layers. I wasn't able to do that for him. But acknowledgement from me as a team leader does give some room to see each other in the function in which we work and to work together within that system.

Identification with a concept or method

A special form of identification is the identification with a method of working or a retail formula. A doctor is identified with an image that has worked for generations. A political party is identified with the concept "*makeable society*". People who work within the realms of coaching and consulting, identify with their method.

This kind of identification is highly motivating. We all know from research in the field of therapy, that after the relationship with your client, belief in your own method is the most important factor of success. The flip side of identification is: *"Mess with my method, you mess with me!"*. For the practitioner of the method it feels like this: *"As the expiration date of the method nears, my expiration nears!"*.

Recognising this pattern

As we have mentioned above, resistance is one good indicator to track down identifications. When sitting down with the person or team who seems to be in resistance, you can address it and ask questions like:

- If I see your resistance as loyalty to something important, what would that be?
- With whom or what are you connected in your resistance?
- On behalf of who else are you, consciously or unconsciously, speaking?
- What was recently, carelessly, lost?
- What shouldn't be lost in or after the transition?
- What don't we see or have we stopped seeing?
- What did we forget to value?
- What do we need to say goodbye to with our full attention?

Other traces of identification require focus on and sensitivity to what isn't being said. It is possibly easier to focus on what is being said but to also listen to who or what is being excluded. What isn't spoken about?

As an inner attitude, you can make use of the natural ability of people to sense when something isn't allowed to be. You don't have to tell a child there is a family secret. A child knows this instinctively. You can use this antenna for 'knowing' to your advantage. Please refer to the paragraph on systemic perception.

People or teams who are familiar with the pattern of identification

- Are sometimes 'not completely present'. The body is present but it is as if they are partially somewhere else.
- Can be a fierce advocate for something: "*You can never touch that, it is sacred, it can't change!*".
- Can be restless or even called a 'lost soul'.
- Can sometimes feel as if they are leading someone else's life.
- Sometimes show behaviour that leads to their exclusion of a group.

CHAPTER 4. PATTERNS

- As a person or team can sometimes show behaviour that nobody can explain: *"Why do we always end up in situation X?"*.

Interventions for identifications

After downsizing in an organisation, there is a lot unrest in a team for foster care. "We have become neurotic", one employee sighs.

"Since the downsize, what isn't allowed to be anymore?", seems to be a question that makes sense.

"Well, we are no longer allowed to work with the biological parents of the children. Only with the children and their foster families."

"So, the downsizing brought about a policy-change causing a group of people, in this case the biological parents, to possibly unintentionally, be excluded".

"Yes, and part of our team is identified with those biological parents, now I get it! Now we can talk to our team about it".

Jan Jacob Stam

The general recipe to trace identifications, is to find out what is no longer allowed to be, what can't see the light of day. Sometimes it helps to wonder when the unwanted behaviour started in the team. Was is immediately after a change or event? It is often necessary to go back into the past once more and acknowledge the incident as well as employees who were in the dark at the time but sensed there was a lot going on.

Leadership requires containment (the ability to let things be for what they were and are) for what once was lost but also and mainly that which is valuable today and won't be around in the future.

4.6.7 Extremes collide

In jargon: Polarities

Polarities is the pattern where two opposite forces are at work.

Opposite forces that summon and exclude each other. The most well-known form of polarities is that of perpetrator and victim. The fact that you have two parents, a father and a mother, can cause polarities. The symptoms of polarities are very identifiable but the link is not always made with the mechanism, the pattern of polarities.

Recognising this pattern
- 'Believing' the opposite of what is needed, for example:
    - oud – new
    - good – bad
    - chaos – structure
    - autonomy – control
    - proactivity – reactivity
    - perpetrator energy/decisiveness – victim energy / passivity
- When there are returning excessive and serious conflicts, even after mediation and interventions, or when the conflicts 'bounce' to a different place in the organisation.
- Becoming completely blocked because of a person or team.
- When a lot of integrators/connectors/mediators are necessary. The integrator could become triangulated.
- When there have to be many a meeting to please everyone: which deeply rooted opposites aren't coming together.

CHAPTER 4. PATTERNS 159

Polarities: connected to two opposite forces that summon and as well as fight each other.

With polarities, it is about forces and not absolute situations. It is about perpetratorship or perpetrator-energy, not about being a perpetrator. It is about victimhood and victim-energy, not about being a victim.

A perpetrator is in a state of being. When we talk about perpetrators, it often seems as if these people are perpetrators for the rest of their lives. Nothing is further from the truth. Many perpetrators start as victims. But also with victims we often think they will remain victims their entire lives. This also isn't true: a victim in a different context can easily become a perpetrator. It is precisely that pattern, where two extremes are inherently connected to each other like an elastic.

Perpetratorship can change into victimhood. Victim-energy can change in to perpetrator energy or summon perpetrator-energy. These energies, perpetratorship and victimhood, can also be present at the same time.

Jan Jacob Stam

In Mexico perpetrator-victim energy is a commonly found pattern. This possibly goes back to the time of the Spanish conquest over the Indian people, or even further back.

In Mexico, there were five managers of a car factory – with a German mother company- who were at their wits end. Together they ran a call-centre with around four hundred employees. All dragging their feet, these call-centre staff members. "What can we do?" the gentlemen asked. "The harder we tug at them, the more resistance we get."

Soon, we came across the pattern of polarities: the managers in the perpetrator-energy and the employees in the victim-energy. But quite frankly, the managers looked like victims. Of all the call-centre staff, no one had turned up, but the managers all agreed that the more they pulled at the employees, the more the employees had a smile on their faces. "What is the quality of the smile?", I asked them. "Triumph" was the answer.

By feeling like victims, the employees felt bigger. They even felt like perpetrators and the managers became victims. There is victimhood in perpetratorship and perpetratorship in victimhood.

Later, I was told that the Spanish conquistadors built cathedrals on top of their Indian temples. The Spanish builders hired Indians because they were good craftsmen. The Indian sculptures made Catholic statues for the cathedral but carved their own religious symbols on the back of them. When, later on they prayed in the church, they openly prayed to the Catholic saints but secretly worshipped their own Gods and Saints.

Three kinds of polarities

We will describe three kinds of polarities. Every kind has a different heritage and requires a different intervention.

1. Between persons or parts of a system
2. In a person
3. Double binds (see paragraph 4.6.8)

CHAPTER 4. PATTERNS

1. Between persons or parts of a system

When there are strong conflicts within a team or organisation or there is strong lethargy than the situation would suggest, this is an indication that polarities are playing a role between individuals or parts of a system. This is caused when within a system, there is one person or group connected to one end of the pole and another person or group is connected to the other end of the pole.

Connected to one or the other pole means that the original opposite forces are either in the past or elsewhere in the organisation, usually at a higher hierarchical level.

As a team member or leader, you can often feel the system energy of this pattern. You sense there is danger but you don't quite understand why. The people that it concerns aren't really dangerous. But still there is something in the air that makes you alert. The way a horse can sense in the herd: *"Somewhere there is a source of danger. I feel it coming through the other. But where, but where…"* You can immediately ask yourself where the suppressed polarities in the system are or wee. Where are or were the strong opposites that exclude each other.

A director of a bank came to us with an issue of two teams who were fighting cats and dogs. One of the two departments' task was to be conservative with money. The other departments' task was to act fast and aggressively when there were currency fluctuations. Both departments were at extreme ends of the polarity. As soon as the director saw this, his tendency to fire both teams disappeared.

Jan Jacob Stam

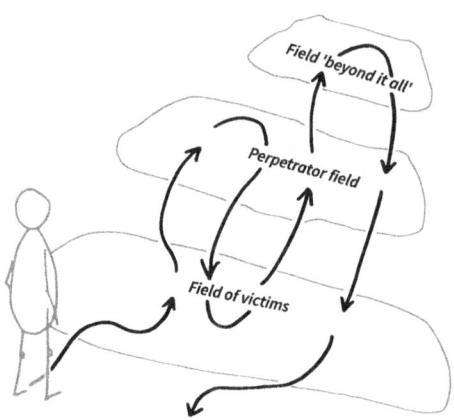

If you want to grow beyond a polarity, you have to accept all aspects of the pattern as equal part of yourself or the team. Then you can grow beyond the opposites.

2. In a person

Polarities can also be within an individual. If there is an unsolved pattern of polarity within one person, it will show itself in strong mood swings. Being a manic-depressive is an example of that. The systemic component of schizophrenia can also be a polarity. For example, because children are born in a marriage between incompatible religions or political convictions or great class differences. Or marriages between descendants of slaves and oppressors, like between originally Dutch people and people from Suriname or The Dutch Antilles.

Imagine, a murder was committed in a family. The event was covered up and it was never spoken about again. This is an, unconscious – invitation to someone in the next generation to be connected to perpetrator-energy as well as victim-energy.

People who know the phenomenon of polarities well, will often find themselves in situations that are highly polarised. In light of their background it could trigger them in such a way that it causes them to perform less. Or, it could be that someone is highly capable in recognising the workings of polarities and able to work with it. These people can also have the unconscious tendency to defend or complement the least strong polarity, as if they want to complete the polarity.

Interventions for polarities

It won't help to want to rid yourself of this pattern. The more you try, the more the pattern will manifest itself. The alternative route is to grow beyond the pattern. This will only be possible if you incorporate the pattern and both poles fully. Acknowledge it as part of yourself or your organisation.

The essence of the intervention is that you, as a person or team, connect to both extremes. Or even stronger, that you become both poles. If you mainly feel connected to the victims, it will be hard to find room in your heart for perpetratorship. If you are more connected to perpetratorship, it will be harder to find room in your heart for victimhood. But those oppressed sides of the pattern are there any way!

We will describe the process the way we have done with a team: 'integrating of and growing beyond the polarity'.

Preparation

You are in a more or less empty room of six by six meters with no tables and chairs. On the floor, three areas are marked. This could be three fields in a line or in a triangle. Label the areas:

- Victimhood (or a different word that fits the polarity)
- Perpetratorship (or a different name that fits the polarity)
- Beyond perpetratorship and victimhood (or beyond polarity one and two)

First phase in the process

All members of the team are invited to take a journey. Start at the same side of the room. This is the present.

Starting from the present, feel what you are most connected to. With the field of victimhood, people on the effect-side of the way things are? Or with the field of perpetrators; people who are on the cause-side of the way things are?

Next, you step into that field. You feel how trusted or strange this field feels to you. Also, feel with how many people you are connected here. People in society, in the past and in the present: people from your organisation, your family… You become aware of everything it has brought you to be connected to this field: your ability to feel who needs something, your ability to protect, etcetera.

After that, you step into the other field. Here, you feel how strange or normal it feels to you. You also feel who else is in this field, people past and present. You may feel some resistance to this field. And which abilities you have developed in the face of this field. Stay here until you can also feel that this is a part of you or your team. Even if it is unpleasant and possibly as betrayal of the other field.

Lastly, step into the field: beyond it all. Here, perpetratorship as well as victimhood have a place. And beyond it. A bigger or wider dimension. Feel what it is like to be here. And what is possible. What abilities can you derive from this field.

Second phase in the process

Proceed by stepping into the different fields at your own pace. More and more, you become the field where you reside. You become perpetratorship, become victimhood, become the dimension beyond it all. Start considering each field as a source, a petrol station. And fill up.

Completion

When you are finished, go to that part of the room where the present is. Become aware of the direction of the future.

End this journey with either a look towards the future or a step into the direction of the future. Know that you can always visit the fields as

CHAPTER 4. PATTERNS

often as you wish... The 'journey' through the different domains of the polarity stem from the insights in the field of Interpersonal Neurobiology (IPNB), partially developed by Daniel Siegel.
In this area of expertise, the starting point is that a healthy nervous system is an integrated nervous system. With integrated they mean that the different parts of the brain, the left hemisphere, right hemisphere and amygdala searching for danger, the narrative memory, the reptilian brain and other parts if the nervous system, meet each other and complement each other when necessary.

A second important discovery is that to a very high age, nerve cells can continue to regrow and can make connections between parts of the body where connection was once lost or never developed. By practicing and inwardly going from one part of the nervous system to other parts, the regrowth of the cells is stimulated. In fact, they start growing immediately.

When Daniel Siegel saw constellations for the very first time in California, his reaction was that constellation did exactly what he had observed as a helpful process in his practice.

From observations and multiple days with interpersonal neurobiologists, we developed the process work as described in 'Integrating of and growing beyond the polarity'.

4.6.8 It will go south if we do it and it will go south if we don't

In jargon: Double binds

**Double binds expresses itself
because something is stuck.**

'Double binds' is a third form of polarities (see paragraph 4.6.6 for the other two).

A woman gives her husband two ties for his birthday, a red one and a blue one. She selected them with a lot of attention and love. Her husband is truly happy with them.

The next day, her husband comes down wearing the red tie. She asks him: *"don't you like the other one?"*.

He is doomed whichever tie he wears. It is impossible for him to do the right things.

Double binds expresses itself when something is stuck. You can feel it. You soon notice that your suggestion for improvement, whatever you suggest, won't work. *"Damned if you do, damned if you don't."*

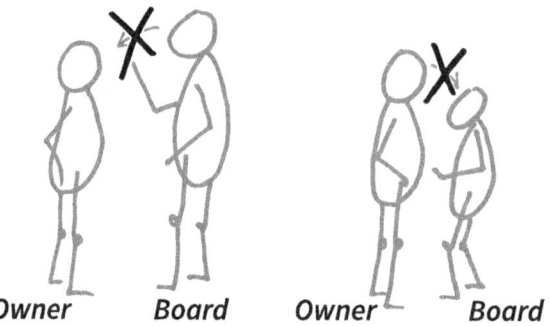

The clamp of double binds: if the board of directors make themselves big, the owners won't accept it, and when the owners make themselves big, the board won't accept it. Two opposite orders working at the same time.

Example

A law firm with multiple offices and many lawyers, was dealing with the following problem. To manage the firm, the partners had chosen a board from among them. As long as everything was going well, everything was going well. In the meantime, because of changes in the market and the crisis, the firm was forced to change the organisational structure. Every time the board made a proposal for change, it was rejected, especially by the partners.

The board and the partners held each other in a steel trap: every time the board proposed a substantial change, the partners, as co-owners, would block any unpopular measures. When the board pushed hard, the partners pushed even harder. When the board was reluctant, they were found too weak. It felt like a clamp with no way out.

CHAPTER 4. PATTERNS

Interventions for double binds

A double bind is a hard nut to crack. It's a strong clamp. Sometimes people try to avoid double binds, for instance by leaving an organisation or keep trying to come up with new proposals. But that doesn't cause the pattern to go away. So far, we have seen three ways to 'solve' double binds:

1. Blow-up the pattern

The first intervention is to blow-up the entire pattern. To make the pattern that instable that it has to fall apart. This requires a certain strength. In the example of the law firm, it would mean that one of the two parties, board or partners has to say: *"we can't keep doing this. We have created a clamp where we are now condemned to each other in such a way that the firm is no longer pro-active and decisive in a market that requires us to be. Let's blow-up the entire construction and start over"*. This is the equivalent of war or crisis, but preferably in controlled way. Collateral damage is however unavoidable. The revenue model is unsustainable, the roles are unsustainable and old securities no longer sustainable.

In essence, this is an explosion of the system.

2. Dig your own grave

The second possible intervention is the opposite of blowing-up the pattern. It is asking all parties to be prepared to dig their own grave. It is asking for the ultimate commitment. Almost beyond the limits of reason.

In the example of the lawyers, it could look at follows: the board could say to the partners: *"As board of directors and co-owners, we ask you the utmost. We ask you to refrain from any expectation you had about the future. The future that is approaching us, looks different to the future we had planned when we created our structure. We anticipated a future together that may not happen. To survive this as a firm, we ask you to let go of your securities, to sacrifice them. And we don't know what we will get in return. What we can do is to stand shoulder to shoulder and not to break up, as we look for a new model or management and action. Are you prepared to do this?".*

This intervention is a conscious implosion of the system. You shrivel up to nothing or something very small. And you ask an enormous commitment to sacrifice what you had and to not fall apart. You ask each other to cut our losses together and to go through the eye of the needle. On the other side, a reality awaits you that may look very different to anything you could ever have imagined. But at the start of this, you won't know that yet.

3. Double binds resolve through 'love'

Jan Jacob Stam

Alexandra is the leader of a start-up in a large accountant's multinational in a South European country. The multinational is so severely stuck in their pattern that they can't seem to be innovative. For this reason, they have made room for start-ups in their company. The start-up quickly grows into 100 employees. Quite a business, but still small compared to the mother company. The moment arises where the innovations, through scale-up, can be integrated in the entirei mother company.

At this moment, the company winds up in a double bind and the developments stagnate:

- In the order, if successful, the start-up takes priority over the mother company.
- If the start-up fails, the mother company keeps their priority over the start-up
- Doomed if they are successful and doomed if they fail. Frustrating and very annoying!

CHAPTER 4. PATTERNS

The leaders of the start-up aren't in a position to blow-up the entire pattern of te mother company. Nor in a position to implode. Those abilities lie only with the management of the mother company. What can Alexandra do? Love the mother company! Love all the patterns. Love everything this company has ever done and does to stabilise the government and society of her country. From a inner perspective, Alexandra has to stand next to the mother company. Not above or below. What she has made as a start-up, they can offer to the mother company. In fact, you hand over the ownership to the mother company without giving up yourself. It is like a marriage. Without prenuptial agreement. Love rises above differences and the interests of parts.

Double binds in change processes

Els is interim manager in a department of a company who produces medical products. There I a lot of cynicism in the male team. The boss, also client of Els, doesn't really know how to deal with the team. Els' energy often 'falls to the floor'.

Jan Jacob Stam

Many change assignments have double bind in them. Openly, the idea is that the leader will be successful but if the leader succeeds, it means that a different part of the system has failed. Or that something is going to change causing it never to be how it was before. That is the hidden brake. You must succeed but you really shouldn't.

There is something striking about Els: her client assigned her as interim manager to the project during a casual conversation "I just came for cup of coffee".

Jan Jacob Stam

Often, both aspects are present with clients: Succeed. And Fail. The unconscious part of the client knóws what he is bringing in by assigning an interim or new leader. The client knóws, without consciously knowing, that the new leader will also undermined the position of the client. The part of the client who acts on behalf of what the system, as a whole, needs, says: *"dig my grave"*. The part of the client that acts from a place of the client himself says: *"Oh shit. What if I am exposed in a bad way?"*.

To Els, ánd to all other clients before change: *"know that the organisation that hauled you in, knows what they have brought in. Even if it was unconsciously. They see and saw something in you, that they didn't even know or realise, that the system as a whole need."*. This is how far their systemic intelligence stretched and maybe even further. Stay with that part in you or with the qualities that their systemic awareness observed. Systemically speaking you are théir leader. Organisationally, they are yóur leader. Be respectful with this double role. Abuse or discovery is punished. Dignity for all is key here. Make sure that you maximise dignity. For everyone.'

When success is impending, I have to break it off…again and again…

4.6.9 Success prevented!

Building a company successfully and then suddenly, just before the summit, something 'happens' or you do something for it all to fall apart. It feels as if true success is not allowed to happen. This pattern looks like a saw tooth.

At its core, this pattern is a variation of the pattern of identifications. During the upward trend, someone is connected to someone, for instance groups from their background who were good in getting things off the ground, possibly with perpetrator-energy. During downward spirals, someone is connected to those who paid a high price for the success of others or for who it was impossible to have success. Something in them says: *"I won't have a better fate than you"*.

Some people make money easily, but can't keep it. In earning money, they might be connected to the perpetrators or with winners in

CHAPTER 4. PATTERNS

their background, and in losing money they may be connected to the victims or losers. Unconsciously of course.

This pattern is found in organisations too. For example, because the founder once brought this pattern to the organisation. Or because the organisation was founded on the remnants of a previous organisation or after a natural disaster. This pattern is also found in societies with a background in slavery.

Interventions for success prevented

When you recognise the pattern, it is relatively simple to ask yourself who you are connected to in the upward trend and who in the downward spiral. Often, becoming conscious of the connection is the first step to untangle it.

> *Sometimes the identification in the downward spiral is very close to home. A successful entrepreneur who came up against this pattern recognises:* "I have an older, handicapped brother. And I realise that something in me has always said: "I will not find a better fate than you"". *And while smiling:* "How presumptuous really, to think that way! As if I would help my brother in any way! And I would almost blame him for the pattern too!".

— Jan Jacob Stam

This is how the unconscious system-conscience and the conscious unit-conscience work against each other.

Organisational topics from a Systemic Perspective

5

In this Chapter, we will discuss some organisational topics. We don't strive to be complete. But we do want to train the 'systemic muscle' a little. And to develop a feeling of what is asked of leadership.

5.1 Innovation

Innovation, starts with a deep appreciation of what there is today. And a deep appreciation for everything that led up to what we find around us today. Think about it, most things we consider outdated were once innovative. We speak of the 'old masters' when referring to Rembrandt and other famous painters. But in fact, they were 'young masters'. In their times, they were young, rash, rebellious and weren't really bothered with what others thought of their work.

Systemically speaking, there is valid reason to renew from a deep awareness that you are building on the foundations of what made the world possible as it is today. If you don't have that appreciation for is here today, or can't manage to appreciate it, that is a good recipe for patterns of what you can't appreciate, will actually come into your innovation. Then it is no longer an innovation but a repetition of patterns from the past.

Often, innovation comes from a different way of thinking than from the way of thinking that caused the present situation, including its problems. In that case, it is 'systemically better' to acknowledge that the problems of today were the best way possible to respond and organise.

5.2 Person and function

Leadership is responsible that every member of the team feels sufficiently part of the team to be able to do his or her job. You can start the day by greeting everybody from a place of: *"Welcome, with everything that you bring"*. *"Welcome as a complete person!"*

So, you don't just welcome the function, but also the person. Of course, this person must fulfil their tasks of their function. If someone is allowed to be there as a person, and not merely as a function, then

CHAPTER 5. ORGANISATIONAL TOPICS FROM A SYSTEMIC PERSPECTIVE

it is less necessary to talk about the weekend for súch a long time. Because sometimes, the exchange about what is going on at home, is an unconscious form of wanting to be seen and acknowledged as a person.

Uniforms, company outfits make the function stronger, and protect the person or close them off a bit. Sometimes that is needed. Try trying on a fire fighter suit with a few colleagues. You can immediately feel the values, the bond of what this profession doesn't just ask from you but also the way you function as óne together.

Brian Eppstein did something important with the Beatles when he took them to a tailor and let them all be fitted for the same suit. Brian: "*I thought, these are four separate boys. It has to be more of a whole. By giving them all the same suit the Beatles became four musicians, one monster and four heads*".

Finding the correct dose of person, function, individual or whole requires precision from leadership.

At a congress of the Dutch Ministry of Transport about the role of government, citizens and other parties in important issues in society, we deliberately made name tags for the participants without their function or organisation on it. We wanted everyone to be there as a Dutchman first, not in their function.   *Example*

I gave one of my employees a new function within the same organisation and the same team. He was partially seconded (50%) with a different company as expert D and remained in his function for the organisation for 50%, but in a new function.   *M.L.*

I spoke to him about how it would be good to have some sort of systemic farewell, for both him and his team and the organisation. The upcoming team day seemed like an appropriate moment because it would be his last day in his 'old' function.

During that day, immediately preceding the break seemed to be a right moment. I thanked him for everything he had given during his work, there was possibly some imbalance and he had given more than received and that he shouldn't forget to take with him that part of him that he had given. I ended with the question to leave as specialist A (his current function) and after the break, to return as expert D (his new function) and that the team would meet him that way.

He left and everyone followed him as it was time for the break. The special thing was, that he was often late to come to meetings but this time he was the first to be back in the room and he really looked different. I welcomed him in front of the entire team with his new function.

5.3 Presence

Someone can be physically present but somewhere else with their attention. Sometimes this isn't exactly conducive for what needs to be discussed or done. Often, you don't know that part of you is somewhere else.

Jan Jacob Stam

Half an hour before I started a seminar abroad with 60 participants, I heard that my wife had had an accident. She fell on the ice, concussion or more? At the start of the seminar, I noticed that my attention was maybe 60% with what I was doing. Of course, autopilot takes over. But to say it out loud to the participants, made it possible for it to be there almost completely. There are organisations who start a meeting with a check-in. Part of the question: "Is there something that prohibits someone to be fully present?". With such a simple question, everybody can become aware of where he or she is inwardly.

When working from home, it is much more important if someone is inwardly with his company than if someone is physically present.

5.4 Which system is speaking? Which system is acting? Which system is listening?

People in organisations represent many systems. We talked about that before. Misunderstandings, mismatches, actions that aren't aligned, can all derive from the fact that different kinds of systems are speaking, without knowing this consciously.

Head of Sales, on behalf of who does he speak? Himself? The frustrated employees in the department? Does Head of sales speak with the voice of clients? An enormous contribution to preventing misunderstandings, is being aware that every one of your colleagues, and you of course, always speak and listen and act coming from a different system. And it is good to ask about it. Are you speaking on behalf of your department or more as member of the board?

5.5 Freeing the function when an employee passed away

When an industrial accident or an accident or illness outside of work, causes an employee to die, it has a major impact on the organisation and the employees left behind. How do you liberate that chair, however painful, for a next colleague?

It helps to take time out together. To reminisce, to hold a memorial, to create a ritual together around the work space of the colleague who just passed or around his or her usual place at the meeting table.

An employee at a production company died. Someone who had worked there for a very long time. The owner asks how he can free the place of this employee again, because a new person to fill the position is needed soon. When I question him a little more, he starts to fidget. "Well, the thing is: the family of the employee has filed a lawsuit against us because they say it was a company accident." An image comes to me and I share it: "Sit on you employee's chair, physically, for a while. Fill-up with the entire story of his history: how he came, what he contributed, what went wrong or didn't work out. And also

Jan Jacob Stam

that which still sticks to the chair. Become the sponge that sucks it up. Then, go see his family and tell them: "I come to you independent of the lawsuit you are filing. I want to tell you what you husband and father contributed to our company. And, strange how it may seem, I want to bring his spirit back to you, because it belongs with you. If you like, I would like to hear stories about him from you". The face of the owner lights up and says: "I now know what to do"."

M.L. *I ask him if he is in a place where someone else left. His body responds immediately. Yes, I came in Chris' place. Do you know how he left the organisation, I ask him? He retired but we didn't really have a farewell party and he was 'done' with his work and the organisation. Especially after the reorganisation, it was really done. He stayed for a while but then retired. The young employee never spoke to him personally.*

I am thinking that this place may not be completely free. I had noticed it before that the way he works often resembles how it was done years ago. Not very innovative while as a person, he is very innovative.

I start explaining to him how it works with places in an organisation that can or cannot be free. I visualise it for him with magnets. How he, as it were, finds himself on top of another magnet and is possibly showing the same kind of behaviours. He is startled and gets emotional. "That is right" *he says.* "The colleague who retired, was nicknamed "bommetje" (small bomb). And they often call me "bommetje" too".

After this, he thanked the previous employee, inwardly, for everything he did. And in thought, he said he would not sit in his place, but will find his own way. He inwardly bowed. I believe (but am not completely sure anymore) he literally even grabbed a different chair. As a team leader, I thanked the employee who had retired inwardly too.

A few weeks later, the employee came to see me to tell me it had really helped. He had more energy and was in his own place and not on the place of "Bommetje".

5.6 The face of competition

Competition sometimes means: wanting to destroy the other person. Then you don't see the competitor, but you see what the competition does to you and your organization. The competitor? is in your system. He gets under your skin, keeps you on your toes and in fact he directs you. With every move the competition makes, a new product, a smart marketing move, your company reacts with: we need to do something even smarter! You are no longer free. You and your competition have in fact become one system. And it is hard to really look at the market when you are constantly having to look at your competition. Eventually, you and your competitor? will be producing more of the same because you are both captured in the same pattern. And in the sub-system that you and your competition are creating, you are each trying to feel better than the other. Or to ignore the other or in a way exclude the other. And as you know by now, the more you exclude something, the more it will come into your system.

Competition can also mean: growth in the face of the other. Together you work in the larger system. You are aware of the position of your competitor in the bigger system. You acknowledge the existence of the other without making yourself bigger or smaller. You and your competition remain autonomous. Two independent systems within the larger field within which you work. This leads to development and growth. Both try increasingly to listen to society. Both try to become a better version of themselves. The answer to your competition is to become better yourself. According to yóur leading principles, and not comparing it to the competition. This makes the leading principles and the expertise of every company increasingly clear. Eventually, the field that you both work in and the market will expand.

5.7 Control

Wanting to be in control, wanting to manage work and the processes is about the future. Often the close future. And about the planned future. To be on top of things again means to have overview. You are at the edge or outside of the system that you want a good overview of and you can rise above it a bit. Think about it, with situations that you have control over, where are you part of the system or on the edge?

Being drawn into a system, without being aware of it, is a good recipe to lose the feeling of control. Sometimes people lose their skills when they are drawn into a system without understanding why they are losing their skills.

If there is something you can do in work situations, it is to watch out if someone isn't being drawn into certain work or a project or another system, without realizing it. Systemic collegiality is drawing their attention to what is happening.

Suddenly, that colleague or employee laughs a lot less. Suddenly, someone looks pale. Or someone's way of walking changes: slower or dragging their feet or in haste and it resembles someone missing the next train. Watch what happens the next time you ask someone how a project is coming along. A change in their voice or emphasis are good reasons to question on.

If it is about control, ask yourself if you have influence on the system you are trying to control. Not having influence and still wanting control is a good recipe for parentification or carrying someone else's responsibility.

A lot of control, checking a lot, looking at the figures daily or following the news can easily give the illusion of control. As if you can influence or change the course of events. This illusion of control over a system you have no control over, is ultimately not healthy. Admitting that you have no control over it is the first step to more control on your own well-being.

This applies to individuals but also for teams and organisations.

For the organisation as a whole, it is also healthy to realise which managers don't have control either. It is no use firing the director of a bank as if he caused the financial crisis. By blaming them or sending them away, doesn't change the system. It makes more sense to realise that we cause crisis together.

People who realise what they do and what they don't have control over, are inclined to find fault for what goes wrong or the force for

CHAPTER 5. ORGANISATIONAL TOPICS FROM A SYSTEMIC PERSPECTIVE

change within their own departments. At least within the system they can influence. Once you know you can't influence the other departments, it is better to say: *"How can we deal with that department differently?"*. In that sentence, giving up control also means giving up our innocence. Checking with yourself which patterns and which behaviors are no longer appropriate with the relationship with other systems outside. You will become unfaithful to yourself.

People who have the illusion if control tend to blame things that go wrong outside of themselves. Someone else is doing something wrong. Unfortunately, you can't change someone else.

Do we have control over evolutionary forces in society and how it influences our organisation? At least not in the way we have influence over the planned future. The only thing we have control over is the way that we deal with the future as it approaches us. It is control by listening well to all the signals that approach us. It is control through being awake. And by recognising the right moment. It also means to temporarily refrain from wanting control of the planned future. The more we want to control the planned future, the less we can meet and observe the emerging future and deal with it appropriately.

Think about the ways in which your company deals with these forms of control. What instruments are used? Are they meant to make up for mistakes in the past, or to prevent the same kinds or mistakes repeating themselves? Are they meant to have a knack for the planned future? Or do they help detecting the emerging future?

5.8 Feedback or Feedforward

We won't go into the rules of feedback, everyone is familiar with those. Let's look at it systemically. Feedback is information from one person about another, from one system about the other. The effect of feedback could be that patterns want to move from one system on to the next. An extreme example is: *"if I were you, this is what I would have done"*. That is imposing my vision of the world on to you, from my system to yours. After all, *"if I were you, I would have done exactly what you did!"*.

The effect of feedback is often to strengthen existing patterns.

Feedback uses either the source of the unit-conscience or the system-conscience:

- from the unit-conscience the feedback I give someone is saying: *"If you do more A, you will belong more; you will fit better in the order".*
- from the system-conscience: *"If you do A, you strengthen the continuity and the patterns that keep our system sustained".*

When in connection with a person's destination, department or company feedforward is in connection with the evolutionary force. The person giving feedforward stands next to the evolutionary force. The giver or feedforward stands shoulder to shoulder with life energy and a person's, department's or organisation's potential.

If you want to give feedforward, connect to the life force that is present but unused. Actually, you don't really concern yourself with the happiness of the person you give feedforward to, but you are concerned with society, customers, people or things that could benefit from that life energy.

In fact, what you are really saying with feedforward is: you can't usurp life energy. Life energy belongs to the emerging future. Life energy wants something of you. What would happen if you followed it? In that sense, feedforward is a ruthless invitation to follow your destination. And of course, there are reasons why this life energy isn't fully flowing yet. And thén you can go back to the patterns of loyalty that keep someone in the place they are today.

Jan Jacob Stam

When I am in a staff meeting, I equally watch myself as I do my colleagues. I am aware when I feel distracted, when I am leaning forward or backward. From time to time, it is a useful intervention to say out loud what I am observing in myself. I also come out and say it when I see something happening with my colleagues. If something

CHAPTER 5. ORGANISATIONAL TOPICS FROM A SYSTEMIC PERSPECTIVE

seems to be wrong in the background, I ask about it. This way, staff meetings have become a lot more in connection with the destination.

5.9 Love and dedication: curse or blessing

The police chief is exactly between two groups of employees, roughly speaking, one group who is willing and one group who is not. Rather large groups because he manages around a hundred and thirty people. "I want to connect them!", he says with so much enthusiasm as well as desperation in his voice. The moment he takes a step aside, the two groups suddenly connect. The chief is stunned. "Your passion to connect them has more of a separating than a connecting effect", I tell him. The chief thanks me over three times during the day for this 'insight'.

Jan Jacob Stam

What strikes me, is that the passion of a manager for the work, for 'backing the employees 100%', in other words for all ways of loving them, makes the employees feel more like children than grown adults, feel more constricted than free and this leads to more division than co-operation. Sometimes love is confining. Should there nót be passion and love? Yes! But what happens is, that all that love and passion is confining when it focusses on that part of the system, organisation or family that you are responsible for. Like the mother gathering her chicks. The fox and her cubs. The team leader and his or her team. Love goes towards the sub systems that you oversee and where you have influence. Side effects of this love is that the sub systems get sealed-off. And who is ín it, shouldn't grow too much.

What is outside the sub systems, soon runs the risk to belong to the 'unpredictable' (or even big bad) outside world. And we defend what is on the inside with our love, against all the unpleasantness that comes in from outside. From the bigger system.

This way, love gets the face of the inflexible, unreasonable, can't-talk-to etcetera.

Systems sometimes ask something that is difficult. When you find yourself in a subsystem, it requires you to love the system around it. The board of directors, management, politics. Especially that part that you have very little influence on. Growth requires you love the outside world. Especially there where unpleasantness comes from If a subsystem wants to be led, self-steering or authoritarian, subsystems want there to be love for the larger systems around it. If that doesn't happen, sooner or later, the system will fall apart in separate sub systems.

Loving also means loving the history of the organisation, your country, the world. It's a little strange to be grumbling about the very organisations and institutions, without whom you wouldn't be or would no longer be alive. That's the same as soiling your own crib, sooner or later tis will turn against the loiterer.

But it is much bigger than that. If a sub system wants to be led, it requires loving the history as well as the larger systems.

If loving focuses on the sub systems, love can turn into hate for the outside world, in conflicts and war.

Is love is focused on the larger systems around us, however imperfect, that love can lead to seeing the essence, to growth and unexpected insights.

5.10 Naughtiness as a source

Jan Jacob Stam

Youssfrey is a friendly looking bearded 63-year-old pharmacist with glasses. Almost 40 years ago, he started a pharmacy chain in Egypt. The chain is collapsing a bit and competition is catching up. Moreover, his old loyal employees are also dozing off a bit and this causes division with the new fresh young employees in the shops. What to do?

To test if his organisation has reached its destination, I as Youssfrey: "How long will you remain on the job?". "Until I die", is his clear answer. The chain also still has a lot of potential, Youssfrey says.

> *A constellation confirms this.*
>
> *"What was, in 1977, the reason to found this chain?" I ask, "Well", Youssfrey says, "We changed the game! Before, for most citizens, pharmaceutical products were hard to come by. It started with one shop close to the people and it grew into a chain".*
>
> *The lights in Youssfrey's eyes don't escape me. I suggests he says the following to one of his loyal employees: "I can't protect you any longer. This company was built on some 'naughtiness'…" A big smile behind the glasses and the beard. "Without you, it would never have become what it is today. But we need some of that naughtiness again."*
>
> *It is incredible how Youssfrey, who has never seen a constellation before, is beaming from ear to ear and looks ten years younger. Apparently, the origins of this company are: be game-changer and a little naughty, still a great resource for changes that are now necessary. Later on, we learned that Youssfrey immediately started making changes in his company…*

Naughtiness is actually a beautiful term to indicate how someone:

- Loves the system that made him or her to what he or she is today
- Ánd knows the limits of what is and isn't seemly
- Ánd stretches these boundaries
- Ánd is fully connected to life energy
- Ánd is connected to the future who wants to use her

5.11 New function

The organisation is growing and more people need to come on board. You need to reflect on what growth really means here.

Growth can mean; more of the same. More students are applying so we need to grow the school. We need more teachers. Those teachers will do what the other teachers were already doing. The function is clear. We need another Math teacher. When the function is clear, you know which person to look for who suits the function.

Growth can also mean: different. A new or different function than we already have, is needed. A new kind of student is applying. Refugees. They need language training. Some are traumatized. A teacher or someone within the team is attracted to, well, to do something useful with this new target group. Figure it out.

Systemically speaking, there isn't a real function yet. It means that everything is dependent on the person to create his own function. We have often see this go wrong. Rule of thumb is that a new function must first be created before you look for a person who could fill this position and to give it form.

A function is never separate from the system. Someone needs to take care of the following:

- that the new function is acknowledged and accepted in the system as a whole;
- that the relationship between the new function and all the other existing functions is clear;
- that the outside world can acknowledge the new function

How does the Dutch teacher relate to language learning of a refugee?

How welcome are these refugees at all at this school?

Does the arrival of refugees change the leading principles of our school?

In short: with growth and a new function there is a lot more to it than with the growth of existing functions.

5.12 Filling the post

If we are dealing with a new function, it is important that the function is given a strong and clear place in the order. Also, the place in the order in relation to the other functions must be clear.

If it is an existing function, then it is important that the chair first be freed. That there was a sound farewell from the previous person holding that function.

These are the next relevant questions to ask:

- What do we need?
- Which systemic function do we need?
- What should the person be other than the one with the qualities to fill in this position?
- Which pattern do we need?

During the interviews with the candidates, focus on the patterns that come up. Ask them!

Investigate for each candidate what the significance is of working in your company or team. What is the systemic function of your company for the candidate? To what extent are you a (replacing) care home: are you that which the candidate can't find elsewhere?

Speaking to multiple candidates can be an enormous mirror for something you missed, or something you aren't consistent or clear about when it comes to this function. Use the interviews to learn about yourself too!

This also means that you can use the interviews to both grow. Not just the candidate you end up hiring, but also for the ones you don't. Make sure both of you go your separate ways with móre. Interviewing is hard work for a candidate. Consider paying him or her for it, not just travel expenses.

5.13 Systemic Competence Management

Systemic competence management means that you use the patterns that you see coming through your employees, for work. This means that you have to know and discuss with every employee what his or her distinctive patterns are. From these patterns stem the situation the employee feels very comfortable in and where he or she feels awful. Don't make a mother's son head of a project group that needs agency. Put a triangulated employee to use in a field of conflict.

Systemic competence management means being sensitive to the destination of the employee. What does life want from him or her? What potential can you see that wants to be used to good cause? How can you create space for it?

Work that suits patterns are good for your colleague and good for the company. It contributes to reliable performance. But be warned that patterns can also be tightening. Work that suits the pattern gives someone wings. But it can also make someone insecure and lead to unpredictable performance. Never a dull moment!

5.14 Cynicism

Cynicism is the phenomenon where people become cold and close their hearts when they are confronted with a misled future. This is often the reason to close their hearts out of self-protection. Prevent the heart from being wounded again. When you meet cynicism, ask yourself immediately: *"What happened in the organisation where people opened their hearts and the heart was wounded?"* Know, that the events could have occurred with present employees working there or in a period from way before. The memory of the organisation is pretty good.

Leadership asks of you to open your heart to people that opened their hearts at the time but also to those who wounded them. Ánd leadership asks of you to open your heart to them, who had to close theirs out of self-protection.

5.15 Skepticism

From a systemic perspective, skepticism is a situation where if you continue with óne more step, your world view might change. Skeptic people are at the verge of their system of concepts. And they feel that if they continue with someone else's world view, they may have to be disloyal to the concepts that were so important to them.

The more you acknowledge that their concepts are important to them, the faster the skeptics will dare to venture into yóur concepts.

To my surprise, it is often the most skeptical participant who at the end of the workshop is suddenly ambassador for a newly presented concept. In their core, skeptics know how important and worthy concepts can be. You don't discard them! Skeptics have a feeling for the essential. The question is how that feeling for the essential can be put to use…

But please don't believe anything we have to say about it!

5.16 Judgments

Judgments attract judgments. Judging yourself or someone else for judging yourself or someone else! It is often felt that it is inappropriate to have a judgment.

Having a judgment about something has a protective effect. So, with someone who judges a lot, you could ask yourself what it is that needs to be protected.

Someone who judges a lot, is (possibly) very loyal to something, for instance a certain value from home, or a certain education or conviction. Or maybe that person in unconsciously connected to someone or a group with that judgment. It is hard work and costs a lot of energy to have judgments. Leadership could ask themselves the following: for who do I work, or does the other person work, unconsciously, in having this judgment. How does having this judgment protect that person?

5.17 Three kinds of 'we' (in other words: cooperating and co-creating)

The notion 'we' is used in different ways systemically. Cause for a lot of drama.

Example

A friend of mine tells me about a week she had on Corsica with her family. When her sister Anna started the day with "What are we doing today?", sister Marieke answered with: "I am going for a walk now". And the family was in confusion. What is that confusion? When Anna says "we", she means the entire family, who are all together at the breakfast table in the holiday home. It is an intervention on the whole. What would be fun and engaging for the entire family?

Marieke, on the other hand, doesn't receive the 'we' as an invitation for the whole but as a word focused on the sum of parts. As a neighbourhood watch says to an adolescent who is biking on the wrong side of the road: "What do we think we are doing?". For Marieke, it is as if Anna has something to say about her when she asks: "what are we going to do?". If you go along with this 'we' the way Marieke understands it, it means you have to give up some of your individual wishes. Logical that you have to invoke your 'I': "I am going for a walk. With my own uniqueness back in place. Just in the nick of time.".

Cooperating and co-creating

Jan Jacob Stam

The penny drops for me. I am not good at cooperating. I have known that for a very long time. But now it is becoming clear to me why. The reason is that I understand the word 'cooperation' in terms of the sum of parts. When I work together, I have to give up something in favour of the others in the sum of parts. I have to give up my speed, others are slower. I have to give up some of my creativity, because I have to explain what I mean before my idea has been fully crystalised. In short; my fear is that I have to compromise on my personality and qualities.

JAN JACOB STAM AND BARBARA HOOGENBOOM

I love co-creating! Then I light up. I understand co-creating as contributing to the whole. And because the whole isn't judged by the quality of my contribution, I can spout out my ideas but also start building something. I simply love being creative with my co-creators. The only thing everybody has to be willing to give up is "it was my idea". The ideas and form and results grow in the whole. The ownership is in the whole and not in the parts.

The potential – 'we'

As an exercise, four of us following a course, do an exercise. The goal is to go for a walk with a horse for one hour. We start as four individuals, each with our own horse on a short rope. Awkward.

After thirty meters, I feel this immense pleasure of becoming one with my horse. Out rhythms merge together and I believe that I adjust my movements to the fluid movements of the horse. After a while, it really looks as if the eight of us have formed one whole. But then something else happened. In the becoming of one whole it seemed as if there was something else, something more than the whole. We connected to potential. The potential of the whole. The future as it approaches us becomes owner.

The horses are heavily burdened by the hornets. At first, we look out for places with fewer hornets. A kind of planned future. Good for the whole.

The moment that potential starts leading us, we no longer pay attention to the question: "where should we go for the horses to have less trouble with the hornets", but we recognize, as we are on our way and when we arrive, which directions are good for the potential of the whole including the potential of the environment.

Even the paved roads we come across, don't hinder us. The machines, neb in orange, the open pavements, damp new roads don't hinder us. The men and the machines and the horses and us trekking (can't call it a walk anymore) all become part of the potential of the village. The potential navigates over and across unexpected and the disruptive new!

Jan Jacob Stam

The next time you say the word 'we', what do you mean?

- We; the sum of individuals
- We; as a whole
- We; as the potential of the whole and the environment?

Have fun with this clarity or confusion!

Transformation

6

Systemically speaking, the essential nature of change and transition processes differs to the process of transformation. In various sections of this book, we have, from a systemic point of view, given implicit indications of what you can run into during change and what it truly asks of systemic leadership.

Change, transition and transformation

We feel, there is much less known about and 'on offer' in the field of transformation. That is why in this chapter, we want to focus on transformation. Not that we can give you any ready-made recipes but we have acquired a lot of insights on what transformation processes demand of leadership. Of course, we will elaborate on both our definitions of change and transition and that of transformation.

With change and transition, we assume that you know where you want to go. Where you want to be after the change. There is a goal or a desired state. Obviously, there are certain systemic questions you can ask, such as:

- Where is the impulse for change coming from? From the outside world? From inside the organisation? From the owners?

- Where lies the ownership of the change? With the contracting authorities? With the leadership team? With the entire team? In the outside world? Ownership is an important theme during change.

- Are the decision-makers in a decisive frame of mind)? During a change process, many decisions have to be made. By management, the owners, the entire team and/or individual employees. But it is useless to change if the decision-making bodies aren't in a situation or state of mind that allows them to make decisions while being in direct contact with the organisation ánd with the outside world.

- Is the organisation changeable? Is the organisation in a situation and 'state of mind' permitting them to make changes and is able to integrate them? If not, it doesn't make sense to start a change process.

CHAPTER 6. TRANSFORMATION

No, we won't go into more detail on change here but want to leap towards another, more extreme form of change; transformation.

Transformation is a phenomenon that requires a lot more than change alone. Transformation demands the utmost of leadership. And yes, the evolutionary force and the developments in the world can be so strong, that transformation is inevitable.

6.1 Elements of Transformation

There are various definitions of transformation. A well-known metaphor is that of the caterpillar into the cocoon into a butterfly. This metaphor works well with, what we mean by transformation.

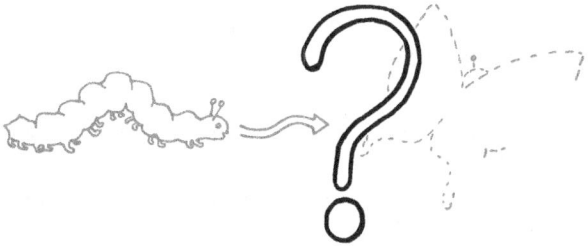

The essence of transformation is that you are going into a process without knowing the identity that will emerge at the end of the process. Systemic leadership will ask itself: what needs to be broken down on the inside for a new creature to arise?

Transformation is a process where, unlike a linear process, you don't know where it will lead to at the end of the process but at the level of identity, something will have changed. You áre something different.

Just to be clear: we know that the caterpillar will turn into a butterfly but the cáterpillar doesn't know this. And the image of the butterfly is romanticized. In transformation processes, it is unsure how beautiful or accepted or viable the new identity is.

There are two important elements in this definition. Firstly, that at the level of identity you are different than before. Not just form but also the essence is different. A butterfly is essentially a different animal than a caterpillar. After a transformation, your organisation is irreversibly changed.

Irreversible: this means that you literally cannot go back to the old form. An important consequence of this characteristic of transformation is that at some point you will reach 'a point of no return'. *"Now we will cross the line, now we will have to let everything go."*

The second element is that you won't know what your identity will be after the transformation process. This means that you can't steer towards reaching certain goals. Goals that are formulated SMART will more likely be in your way than be helpful.

All those processes, where you know where you want to end up, and that counts for most of them, we classify as change, development or transition. If you want to reach a goal, it is mainly that goal that gives you direction during the way.

The consequence of this element of transformation is that where you want to go, the goal, no longer provides any guidance. You merely have the process. The rest is unsure, sometimes terrifyingly so. And this process sets a high standard for leadership. We will name a few here. Again, we will let ourselves be directed by the three survival mechanisms of social systems: surviving the unit, surviving the system as a whole and Evolutionary force. We will see that these three survival mechanisms often overlap in the transformation processes.

What strikes us most is that there are very few teachings for transformation processes. For changes going from A to B, there are many instruments to help navigate the process. For transformation, this is limited. That is why, in this chapter, we have a limiting set of leads to offer. It is a field in development and to which the systemic perspective can contribute hugely.

6.2 The Unit Conscience

A wake-up call

The impulse for transformation often comes from the Evolutionary Force. Many different kinds of organisations and structures that held society together and served society well, are approaching their expiration date. Problems can no longer be solved with the same way of thinking that created them or with the consciousness within which the problems arose. And the way of thinking or the consciousness that is needed, is simply not yet known.

The future, as it approaches us, is starting to rock existing organisational structures. Not because they aren't good but because they are finished. They have fulfilled their function.

When in the nineties, the Dutch Housing Cooperatives had finished their task of building affordable housing for large groups of people in society, they didn't 'know' what to do. Dissolve themselves? Convert into something else, maybe a Developer? The latter happened often.

The call for transformation can be sudden, from a crisis or a war. But also, for instance, with an enormous influx of refugees travelling across countries or an entire continent, natural disasters or rapidly developing technologies that radically changes the behaviour of consumers. Think of development in online sales that turned Retail on its head.

The call for transformation can also be insidious because society changes. As with the Housing Cooperatives, it is important to listen to the early signals. The call will first be the whispering of the wind, slowly swelling into the roaring of a storm.

What Systemic Leadership asks of you, is to listen well to that call from the Evolutionary Conscience, from the emerging future that the survival and the identity of the organisation, as it is today, is at risk. Being aware and facing the fact that adjusting, tweaking and changing will no longer fundamentally help, is an act of courage.

Closing the business down can be a good and dignified solution. Closing an entire school system or closing down government is a different story. Although... it could be interesting to see what would happen if those systems would simply be closed down.

An alternative to closing down is to venture into a transformation process. Preferably, this is an active decision. A moment to mark. The reasoning being that it gives you the possibility to meet the requirements of a transformation process as best you can.

6.2.1 The principle of Belonging, during transformation

Commitment

Commitment is all about the future. Commitment is a special way of belonging. Commitment is the agreement to belonging in the future, without any security that on the other side of the black hole, there will be room for everyone.

Jan Jacob Stam

Frank is a fire chief who has been trying to change his organisation from a rule and control based organisation to a value based organisation. What may strike you immediately is that a goal is defined here but there are also some transformative parts to this process. It requires the employees to let go of something that provided them with an anchor for so long, without knowing what this value-basedness will give them in return. Moreover, as it turns out later on, the whole process of the Fire Brigade is embedded in society's need for safety. Most likely, providing safety as we know it over the past seven decades, is an illusion.

Frank joins us because he has a question about a specific issue within the organisation. Soon, we start talking about the organisation as a whole. It feels as if, together, they are approaching a point of no return. Frank notes that, although the organisations' principles driven by craftsmanship, connection and trust may have great support within the organisation at large, at this time, too much is being asked of the individual employee. They are asking everyone to let go of

CHAPTER 6. TRANSFORMATION

some of the values that were very important to people in the organisation. And it is proving hard.

Intuitively, I ask Frank how long he will be staying. He says: "As far as I am concerned, I don't have to leave at all". When I imagine what this might mean to an employee, it makes me insecure. I mention this to Frank and add; "If you would say "I will stay", as an employee, it would help me let go easier". "You have a point", Frank says, "I have never said out loud that I will stay". "Yes", I say, rubbing it in, "You should not only say this on the inside but to the outside as well. To all commissioners in the fire protection district and to society".

Of course, Frank doesn't know if, during the next half of the process he may lose his job, that could happen.

During transformation processes, it is of great importance that the leader remains in his position from beginning to end. All too often leaders back down. The entire process and employees then stay behind devastated. If you are not willing to stay for the long haul, don't start. That is commitment.

"I will stay." *Example*
"As long as it is given to me, I will stay."

There is another catch to this. If a leader successfully follows through on a transformation process, chances are he or she will become popular demand for other organisations. Also, here, the commitment is "*I will stay*".

You often see this kind of commitment amongst firefighters within the Fire Brigade. "*We will stand shoulder to shoulder, until death do us part.*"

Quirks and shadow sides

Despite standing shoulder to shoulder, transformation processes often mean that the organisation can end up in survival mode. This means that all sorts of fight and flight impulses will appear. Saying "*I will stay*", means that I have sealed off the emergency exits for me.

But how about the fight-impulse? This will most certainly emerge. Furthermore, it can be chaos during a transformation process. What was always either distinctly good or bad before, is now unclear. Be prepared that people's quirks will start seeing the light of day. These quirks are all about survival. Survival of the person. Or a survival mechanism unconsciously taken on from the family or societal system. What is more, these quirks will and should emerge. You can prepare yourself for them.

Jan Jacob Stam

Four directors of a very large bank in Brazil are fully aware that in a year, they will all have different positions. That's the way things go after Presidential elections: a new President means a different political persuasion and all the management posts are replaced or exchanged.

Their concern is how to manage the bank during the coming year in such a way that they can maintain the continuity of the bank. So that, as management, they work as a whole instead of a fragmented sum of parts.

A very simple intervention was to let every manager choose a representative for their 'quirky self'. They introduced and acknowledged this 'quirky self' to each other. That is the moment when they knew, predicted, that this "quirky self" would show itself often during the process to come. But now they would recognise it.

Six years on the managers still talk about how acknowledging one's own and each other's' shadow sides had helped them to stick to their commitment.

6.2.2 The principle of Exchange, during transformation

During transformation processes the show must go on. There needs to be systemic exchange even though it's nature changes.

> *TomTom sends me a letter to announce they won't be making anymore map-updates. A slight shock to me as frequent user. But of course, they still need to try to keep the client-supplier relationship. Or, if that isn't possible, to find different ones.*

Jan Jacob Stam

This example immediately outlines the problem. If you open yourself to the force of evolutionary development, you don't know what products and services you will be offering in the future. Nine out of ten start-ups, companies that offer a new product or service, seize to exist within two years. It is an art to understand both the call for the finite nature of something as well as the call for something new. Even if you don't yet know what the new product or service is going to look like. Marc Wesselink, one of the leaders of Bootcamp Amsterdam: "*The biggest difficulty for people of start-ups, is to waive their prejudice. Prejudice about how the world works*".

Prejudice is all about the planned future, a start-up is all about the emerging future.

The price

There is another aspect to the principle of exchange. In the future, someone or something will have to pay for the transformation. Not all clients that were served will remain being served. Not all positions and employees will have a place in the organisation. There will be damage, there will be trauma's.

Right at the beginning of the transformation process requires leadership to face that a price will have to be paid. Obviously, there is hope that the societal gains will be greater, and the final balance will be positive. But that doesn't prevent that leadership requires that, beforehand, you look those, who have paid a heavy price, straight in the eyes. Even if you don't yet know who they are.

6.2.3 The principle of Order, during transformation

In a transformation process, the principle of Order seems to dissolve. Age, order in positions, even order in leading principles, everything seems to become fluid. This means that a lot of grip is lost. Order is the principle that provides the most support in a stable organisation. Holding on to order as a lifeline will stand in the way of a transformation process.

Instead of order, commitment to stay together comes first, so the principle of belonging, as a mechanism to remain a whole. Subseiquently, new products and services will move new patterns, new leading principles and a new order in positions forward out of the chaos.

6.3 The System-conscience: Survival of the system as a whole

The system-conscience has always taken care of the unconscious patterns that have sustained the organisation and have made the organisation predictable. Predictable means that it is pretty sure that the planned future indeed will become "*true*". Tomorrow the sun will come up as well.

The system-conscience will do its utmost to maintain these patterns when a transformation phase is in sight. Employees will become identified with these patterns. The outside world, too, will try to put the organisation in its place with their opinions and even complaints and blame. Public opinion is a good recipe to restrain an organisation that is potentially ripe for transformation, like education. The more we think education is deteriorating, the more images we have about what it should look like and hence the harder the transformation process will be.

What is asked of leadership here, is to embrace all patterns and all

CHAPTER 6. TRANSFORMATION

the good reasons for those patterns and the fact that things will never go back to what they are.

Letting go of patterns mainly requires the following: to very much acknowledge them. Possibly all those patterns that, ever since the foundation, have maintained stability and progress.

Systemic Sentences

Leadership also requires a great understanding of the hidden systemic sentences in an organisation, branch or society. In the example of Frank, the Fire Brigade and fire protection districts; they (and all of us) are dealing with a deeply rooted systemic sentence in Dutch society. A sentence from government to civilians: *"Please, go to sleep now. The government will watch over you"*. A striking amount of people remember the context in which this sentence was expressed. And what happened a few days after: World War II started for the Netherlands with the bombing of the heart of Rotterdam.

If this systemic sentence is true, then the result is that government takes on the responsibility and, unconsciously, civilians take on the expectation, that there will be safety. And that safety will be provided by government. Perhaps, this sentence is ready for acknowledgment and review.

A documentary about Israel tells us how civilians play a major role in safety during terrorist attacks. "When civilians see something untoward, together, they can tackle an attacker at a very early stage. If necessary, they are prepared to put their own lives at risk. If we would wait for police or army to arrive at the scene, it's often too late. It's a matter of attitude." — Example

---

Good Advice

In transformation processes, there is also the element of transfer to the next generation. This, being independent of it truly being a next generation or a different subsequent element.

Unconsciously, good advice from one side of transformation processes to the other, are meant to lift patterns over and across the transformation and infect the old patterns into the new system. Therefore, refrain from good advice. Befriend the Not Knowing.

6.4 The Evolutionary Force

The evolutionary force provides us the future as it approaches us. It differs essentially from the planned future. During change processes, you are mainly planning the future as a kind of landscape that lies before you. The 'only' thing you have to do is to make sure the landscape actually takes form. The planned future is of great importance. For a large part, it has sculpted society and its achievements as we know it today. Many large, established organisation offer security and guidance in this planned future. Moreover, we try to make the planned future 'good' for those concerned.

The future as it is coming towards us, the emerging future as we call it in this book, is produced by the evolutionary conscience. The evolutionary conscience is a larger force that takes the world, she causes war as well as peace, light as well as darkness, crisis as well as prosperity. The effect of the evolutionary force is that, after a period of disruption, it brings society back to calmer waters. But how that water feels, looks, or which countries can be administered, we don't know.

Not knowing yet recognising

Leadership during transformation processes requires a special quality. It very much requires that you let go of the need to know what the organisation will look like áfter the transformation. Ánd it requires the ability to recognise that you have arrived. You know it's right.

Leadership also asks of you to work in service of the Greek God Kairos, the God of the right moment. You can't plan what the right moment will be to intervene in a transformation process, but you cán recognise when the right moment presents itself. And then to not hesitate. But to act. Or better said: let yourself act.

CHAPTER 6. TRANSFORMATION

If you expose yourself to the evolutionary conscience, you know that the future will be shockingly different, but not hów. The invitation made to leadership is not just to expose yourself to the evolutionary force but to become part of it. Moving from someone who endures it being an actor in it. A tool in the hands of the evolutionary force.

Once you have been there, in the land of the evolutionary force, it is also good to return to the planned future. To Kronos, de God of the step by step planning. Often, the planned future looks different once you have been to the emerging future. The art of controlled chaos, is to have Kairos and Kronos work together in the right way.

It may be clear by now what it means to be a leader during transformation processes: leadership doesn't lead by standing alongside the process and directing from that position. Leadership gives up its own secure position, becomes part of the transformation process and lives the transformation from that position. In a way, leadership merges and everyone is equal.

Destroyer and Creator

You can only build if you can destroy. And that definitely goes for transformation processes. In fact, destroying and the willingness to destroy comes before building. And worse: it is about destroying something you possibly built yourself.

It is striking how much destroying is part of the fashion industry. I saw that in the fashion industry in London, when I worked there. To make space for innovation, you need to destroy what you created today. That pattern was visible in the entire branch. The symptom they were suffering from, was that management was volatile and never stayed in position long. The pattern of the branch had transferred to the organisation itself.

Bert Hellinger is one of the few authors who says: "Some of those books I wrote can be destroyed…" It sounds so simple, but if we truly feel what he is saying, it asks for deep respect. How much room do

Jan Jacob Stam

you create for the emerging future if you are willing to destroy all the products of your heart, soul, love and brain!

What do I want from life: what does life want from me?

From the perspective of the planned future you can think in terms of: What does our organisation want to be in the future. What significance do we want to give to society? In other words: What do we want from life? With the planned future as your starting point it is easy to think we are owners of life. That we can do with it what we want or what is useful.

From an evolutionary force' perspective, your thoughts are more in terms of: What does life want from me? What does the life force of our organisation, as it flows towards us, want? What if we go with the flow and open ourselves up to what the life force, flowing through us, has in store for us?

Leadership in transformation processes means giving up ownership to the emerging future. To that which life wants from us.

6.5 Ba and Ya

From what inner place do you lead?

Transformational leadership asks a lot of the unit-conscience, the system-conscience and the evolutionary conscience. Leadership demands you undergo these processes yourself as well as being able to contain it for all those involved.

Leadership also requires containment across time. An important question here is: From what inner place are you leading? From the past? From the present? From the planned future? From the emerging future? Passed the emerging future?

Often, we aren't aware of the inner place where we reside and from which place we act. But it has enormous influence on how the process is lead ánd experienced.

CHAPTER 6. TRANSFORMATION

> *In retrospect, I realise that as a 22-year-old teacher to my 16-year-old students, I tried to teach my students what was relevant when I was 16. However much I thought I was teaching them from the future, at the time I was working with a very progressive project-based learning, I was still teaching from the past. The inner place of the past.*

Jan Jacob Stam

What is Ba and what is Ya?

'Ba', is a Japanese term that you could translate to: the origin of everything. It is the connecting point from which the differentiation, as we know it today, originated.

Looking at the influx of refugees from the Middle East towards Europe, the Ba-point, the origin of this large movement, is probably from fár before the Crusades. Maybe even the moment when the divisions in the great world religions started.

A Ba-point can also lie closer.

> *For example, for a successful Spanish company, that point was on the day that the founder heard that his company had gone bankrupt ánd that his wife was pregnant. He scratched his head three times and thought: "Life must be different". He founded a Charity.*

Example

If you want to understand how an organisation is todáy, it is good to know this Ba-point. It is kind of a mini Big-Bang from which all the essentials of the company can be understood and explained. By default, Ba lies in the past. 'Ya', means: 'That, where it can all lead to'. A point of convergence. In the future. At least passed the planned future.

> *When Bert Hellinger once worked with a woman from Bosnia, the woman said at the end: "The former Yugoslavia has fallen apart".*

Example

> *"Yes, for a while", Bert said with a mysterious smile. Hellinger can only make a comment like if he is in a Ya-point.*

Ba is a Japanese term. 'Ya' was born out of Ba. B is the second letter of the alphabet, Y is the one before last.

Being between 'Ba' and the present:

- founding of the organisation
- growth
- moments of stagnation
- despair
- almost giving up
- incidents
- in short, all occurrences that marked and made the organisation.

Between the present and 'Ya' are:

- founding of the organisation
- all plans, short and long term, in short, the planned future
- the emerging future as it comes towards us, from all sides
- the future still unknown successes and incidents
- trauma's that the organisation will cause, that which the organisation wants to transform into.

Why are these abstract and philosophical concepts so important to transformation?

CHAPTER 6. TRANSFORMATION

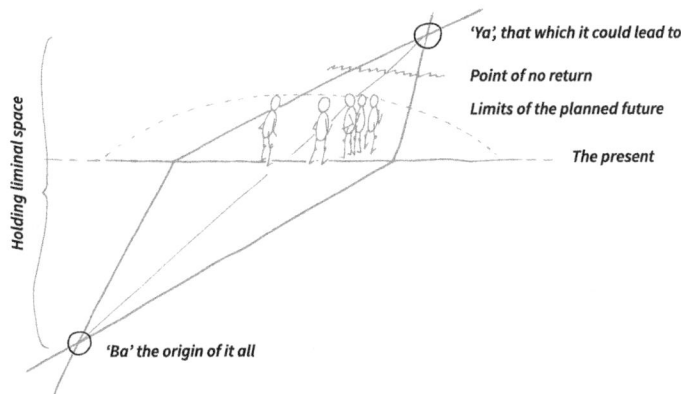

Transformation requires leadership to span from the origin, 'Ba' to that which it could possibly lead to, 'Ya'. Holding liminal space, at the point of no return.

Ba and Ya, and everything in between, are positions from which you can look and act. They are all sources. A developing system responds differently to leadership from different positions.

Below, is a rather long example of a constellation where the person asking the question, takes the 'journey' from Ba to Ya. The example illustrates what can happen if someone makes the journey from Ba to Ya. For now, this is the best way we let you experience what the effect is of this process through text in a book.

Jan Jacob Stam

Cherry, who has slavery in her family history, lives in London and takes care of a terminally ill woman and the woman's 2-year-old son. The young mother, the woman, comes from an Old English imperialist heritage, is wealthy and lives in a centuries-old house, that has known much disease and death. Cherry wonders how, in the constellation, she can best place herself in relation to the family. We map her question in a constellation.

The constellation

A representative for the house, slavery and for the terminally ill woman is set up. And for her son. It is immediately apparent that the house also represents Imperialism.

With that, we have a field in which an axis is formed by slavery and imperialism.
The representative of the terminally ill woman retreats to the side of the field where the future has a place.
Cherry stands up and, with all her heart, embraces the representative of slavery.
"There is so much love stored in slavery", escapes my mouth. The representative of the terminally ill woman has no longer retreated but looks up at Cherry and slavery.
At this point, we invite a representative to the field for 'that where it all came from'.
This 'Ba'-point represents the shared origin of what is taking place here and now. A kind of mini Big Bang, by nature a moment from before imperialism as well as slavery existed.
We try not to go into images or specifics of what this could be in a more concrete history of mankind.
Cherry moves, thoughtfully, slowly towards this Ba-point.
She looks it in the eye and consents.
That is what it looks like.
Later she tells us: "When I looked it in the eyes, I saw the separation of the country, the fear to survive and the rivers of blood that we created in our existential panic".
Next, Cherry slowly crosses the axis of slavery-imperialism towards the future.
Then, I invite her to go to the point 'where it could all lead to': the Ya-point.
The Ya-point is somewhere in the emerging future, the future coming towards us.
Cherry moves in that field and remains there for a while.
She says: "For me, this place is full of life and I enjoy being there. I am also very aware that the needs of the slaves have been met, so I don't project and anger towards my client, the terminally ill woman. I some way, I need their permission to continue, to be sure things will happen in the correct order".
The representative of slavery consents.
In the meantime, the representative of the son follows Cherry's every move, while the representative of the mother is sitting on the ground, turned inwardly.

CHAPTER 6. TRANSFORMATION

> *I invite Cherry:* "Maybe after this journey, you can look at the mother and her son with new eyes. And maybe you could tell the son about it, without words".
> *Cherry:* "I imagine that I am holding him and that, together, we acknowledge the heritage of our ancestors and the impact of slavery. I imagine that I show him all the women that will keep him in the world, will embrace him, after his mother dies. I see us together when he is a young man and he tells of the stories of our ancestors by a camp fire, from an inner place of deep empathy and compassion. It becomes 'our' story and we tell it together".
> *Minutes later, she says:* "I have the feeling that the movement between Ba and Ya was a moment of no return. We can't go back after having seen all this and it is a hopeful and beautiful feeling. We agree with this emerging future, all of us… and so now we jump into this potential future". *A future where descendants of slaves and slave owners heal the collective wounds together and where we reclaim humanity.*

In later situations, we invited leaders to make a same journey. We then asked them to be aware of which interventions they would make at the different moments and positions in the process from Ba to Ya.

What hás become apparent, is that solely working from Ya, without embracing and encompassing the entire history, from Ba to the present, evokes a lot of resistance in the organisation. It looks like the entire arch from Ba to Ya needs to be carried. Curiously enough, the more that happens, less we need to think in terms of past, present and future. It is as if the line of time folds together into now-ness.

6.6 Holding Liminal Space

How, as a leader, can you make sure that you create a safe space for the entire process of transformation? Maybe you have heard of it: holding space. Holding space is about creating a holding in which transformation become possible.

Holding space is a state of leadership where you embrace the entire organisation that is in transformation. It's a form of 'agency-force' (see paragraph 3.1). You make a kind of visual or energetic ring around the entire system. A ring that is transparent and permeable. Influences on the inside can go outside and influences from outside can come inside. As needed, the tap of permeability opens or closes somewhat.

Inside the ring of holding space, everyone is welcome the way they are. In a way, everyone is equal.

Once you have made the ring of holding space, you can inwardly retreat a little more. And as you retreat, your attention becomes stronger. As you retreat, the rind of the holding space becomes larger. The way you stretch an elastic.

The larger the holding space, the more insecurities people within the holding can deal with. Please note: prevent a false sense of safety. Don't become the protecting father or mother of the organisation and the people in it.

Holding space is not about what you do, it's about how you are. It's not a quality of doing but a quality of being.

Holding liminal space has an extra dimension. The word liminal is derived from the Latin word Limen: threshold. The threshold after which there is no return.

Leadership requires having one leg on one side of the threshold and one leg on the other. Holding liminal space means to herd the process where people are approaching and crossing the point of no return. Internally, you are on both sides, including everything that makes people want to remain before the threshold and everything that makes people want to cross the threshold quickly. It means you are prepared to embrace not only joy but also junk and dirt.

As people approach and cross the point of no return, they are confronted with their deepest self. And further to that, what it means to be human.

So, don't start a transformation process if you are not prepared to be confronted with ánd to endure the deepest selves of those who are involved.

6.7 Facing future trauma

It's almost unavoidable, in a transformation process you will cause i trauma responses. With employees, clients or in society. This comes very close: If you work in a process of urban regeneration, you know something will have to be torn down. This tearing down will be traumatic for some people.

With traumatic we mean that áfter the process people won't be able to return to their original force and life energy. The team ends up in survival mode. This often goes hand in hand with separating important traits, such as the ability to trust or the ability to make decisions. A side-effect of a trauma-reaction is that a team or organisation becomes fragmented. Suddenly, everyone is lonely and no one can reach each other.

During the process of transformation, you will also encounter so-called reactivations. It has become apparent that organisational systems have a solid memory. Separate from the individual memories of people who work in the organisation. How the memory of an organisation or a societal system exactly works, we don't know. But we do know it's there and it can sometimes prove difficult in the process.

Reactivations are the phenomenon, that when a system or a person approaches a situation similar to a traumatic event in the past, the system or person will respond in the same way as before. It expresses itself through extreme resistance and /or panic attacks that seem much more forceful than you would expect, given the nature of the process you find yourself in. It is helpful to recognise reactivations. In any case, leadership requires the preparedness to address and acknowledge the earlier traumatising event. Storytelling helps with this.

What also helps, is to allow people to connect to their roots. The more people are allowed to connect to their roots, the less they suffer from dramatic and disruptive events. People can always inwardly carry their own roots, in their faith, their countries or place of birth. Inwardly, because it is not always possible to stay connected literally.

Lastly, it is always good to keep your options open in transformation processes. The reason people suffer during dramatic events is the fact that they don't have ány options. That's why they go into survival mode. Options should be three or more. One option doesn't count as choice. Two options are a dilemma. Three options or more provides inner space and peace.

6.8 Transformative Phase

In the same way water can be in a state of ice, snow and water, an organisation can also be in different states (phases): Stabile, developing, changing, in a state of dissolving, in transformation. Leadership knows different kinds of transformative interventions: first, second and third order interventions.

6.8.1 First order interventions

First order interventions are interventions where leadership offers solutions. A team has a problem and you solve it for them Very useful, especially when swift action is needed.

6.8.2 Second order interventions

With second order interventions, you take a detour. Leadership, firstly, investigates what the problem is a symptom of. What is the absenteeism trying to tell me? Which underlying patterns want to come to light? Second order interventions are focused on uncovering the underlying mechanisms. It means the team doesn't walk away with solutions but with insights. The team have to translate these insights into action themselves.

When a team understands that the tensions and losing each other has to do with a reactivation, you don't necessarily have to organise team meetings to get people to connect again. You trust the self-healing capacity of the team and the creativity to find a what works for them, after understanding the underlying mechanisms that estranged them from each other.

What a system mainly needs are facts. Even if the facts, to our standards seem nasty or unkind. A social system, the system conscience, isn't interested in good or bad. Notions of good and bad originate from the unit conscience. You do something that according to the unit, the organisation, family, faith, country, the law is considered 'you no longer belong'.

Systemically, justice doesn't exist. Righteousness and justice refer to a 'Big Brother', the law that says one behaviour is 'good' and the other is 'bad'. These are concepts of the unit-conscience.

In a board of directors, people have been suspended: the chairman, being the managing director and later a division manager. Initially, the other members of the board filled in the blanks but later decided they wanted to deal with past events. The symptoms they named amongst others were: 'not being able to let go of the work', 'complaining about each other', and 'being inner focused'.
"We just want to know what really happened", one of the directors from the team says. Unsuspectingly, her wish panned out differently than how she meant it. "We don't know why the managing director was suspended. Moreover, we are not allowed to talk to him", she added.
Moments later, it turns out that the entire organisation was under severe criticism and a journalist was conducting research. After the managing director was suspended, the other directors set up an internal investigation, if anything, to be ahead of the journalist. Research showed that too many unacceptable things were happening in the division of one colleague. Two members of the team insisted the manager in question to report these occurrences to higher management. The manager did and was suspended immediately.
"Mmm, you basically forced your colleague to betray himself", I say out loud. They are startled and start bringing forward arguments as

Jan Jacob Stam

> *to why they did it. This is where the system conscience doesn't soften up. It is interested in facts. Not in arguments or accountability of facts. We ask someone to be representative for the suspended division manager in a constellation.*
> *I ask the friendly colleague, who had had the conversation with the division manager and had advised her to come forward and go to higher management, to come forward and to say to the representative: "I did it".*
> *Full stop, nothing more, nothing less.*
> *First, he tries, "I did it, because..." but everyone could feel that that wasn't going to work.*
> *Then, clearly and distinctly, he says: "I did it".*
> *Then another colleague stands up and says: "I want to say that too". And he does.*
> *These words were the beginning of a not so easy but cathartic process.*

The colleague that started the meeting with "*I would like to know what exactly happened*", got something in return in a different way than he probably expected. In fact, at the end of the constellation, he can put aside all his opinions and start living with the fact that he will probably never know the exact arguments for the suspension.

The biggest effect of this process is that everyone in the team including the suspended director, can look each other in the eyes again. It is because they were prepared to surpass the truth of the unit-conscience (Who is right? Who is in his/her right?) towards the truth that the system conscience desires.

A system wants to be whole

After the first, cathartic process, a second part can follow.

Of course, the suspension was also traumatising for the team. To survive this, they had given up a few important abilities.

One by one, symbolically, they retrieved these abilities and connected to them. "*I gave up my creativity. And now I take you back. Give me the chance to reconnect to you." "I gave up the ability to learn. I take it back." "The ability to sometimes not know."* Etc. etc. etc. Emotional yet precious. Especially when the members of the team introduced their abilities that they had given up, to each other. *"This is my creativity. I had given it up. I now introduce it to you. When I reconnect with my creativity, it might be awkward, but help me when I do."*

Writing them down, these sentences sound theatrical and absurd. But in the moment, they were very normal for this team.

They had the courage to be vulnerable enough for processes like these. Also, because they felt that the whole, called team, wanted to continue as a whole. Including the suspensions as inextricable part of their history together. And more than the sum of parts.

6.8.3 Third order interventions

Third order interventions are interventions that bring a team or organisation in a transformative state. The interventions are aimed to:

- realise that a process is about to start, where we aren't sure how we will come out of it at the other end
- creating conditions for commitment
- creating conditions where it will be acceptable that original hierarchical positions will no longer be an automatic basis for power and authority
- there will be holding space for the processes where at some point there will be a point of no return
- People's deepest being, including all the junk, is allowed to be.

What these interventions will look like depends on the present state of the organisation, individuality of the organisation and the extent of transformation that will be required.

Jan Jacob Stam

The question eleven midwives from Uruguay have is, now that they are growing as an alternative form of Birth care: "How can we integrate in, or work together with the existing systems in health care. How should we organise ourselves now we are growing fast and are a network to be reckoned with? And how can we be financially independent".

The origin of this practice is found in rebelling against the mainstream forms of Birth Care. The form of Birth care that they offer is based on Birth care the way it is normal with the indigenous people.

These eleven women have brought to this session:

- *A Gynecologist, who works for a large regular hospital as well as for this organisation of midwives*
- *A General Practitioner, who refers to both mainstream health care as well as this practice*
- *A Yoga teacher*
- *A Haptonomist, who is affiliated to the midwives and works with parents-to be*
- *A parent, who is both client of the practice and has taken up the role of manager in the practice*

In short, not only did the midwives come, but they brought part of their context. Later, it proves to be an important prerequisite for their transformation process.

We start by giving everyone the opportunity to voice their thoughts on this issue, how we can connect more to or be of more service to mainstream Health Care. The fear of giving up what they have, the possibilities there are, everything passes in review. And everyone listens and accepts. They start to contain each other's' situation without wanting to protect or patronise. Not being able to ask for money for their services, because birth is a natural process. The apparent appeal of their work, that makes them grow and their network formula isn't sustainable. The desperate manager. Who tries but fails to keep the business running financially. Everything is given a voice.

CHAPTER 6. TRANSFORMATION

As we progress, you can sense that a transformation is on its way. This means that the possible price has become negotiable. "If we change, I don't know if I can stay", the yoga teacher says.

Slowly, commitment grows to take this process on together. And to keep the price in mind.

A systemic intervention shows how their 'passion for their vocation' almost shuts out the principle of being 'economically viable'. They find themselves in an or-or deadlock, a double-bind. It becomes clear that they need to grow beyond this contradiction, before they can start thinking about an organisational structure of a cooperation with mainstream health care institutions.

The intervention ends with every party concerned connects to 'passion for the vocation' as well as with 'being economically viable'. They even dare to become it a little.

The eleven women feel seen, acknowledged as people and professionals. They can see each other as a whole and they can see where the whole, the midwives practice, wants to move towards. And they can see the gynaecologist, the GP and representatives of mainstream health care. They can be seen.

It is clear: they leave the session in a transformational state. On their way.

Two months later they let me know, through a joyful skype call, that the government of their country has asked them if they would like to play a larger role in the development of Birth care in their country. They hadn't even been actively pursuing that. Apparently, they created the space in which the emerging future was welcome.

More from these authors

Systemic Coaching

Jan Jacob Stam and Bibi Schreuder
In Systemic Coaching, Jan Jacob Stam and Bibi Schreuder talk about how you can apply systemic work in a coach setting. Not as a responsible leader but more from the side-line position that a coach often has. The book includes many tools and processes and encourages you to apply systemic work. This book was also translated into Spanish as 'Coaching Sistémico'. Other translations are in the making.

Wings of Change

Jan Jacob Stam
I this book, you will read how systemic principles work in an organisation. You are visiting, and Jan Jacob gives you a tour through various different organisations, and as an experienced tour guide in this field, will tell you all about what he finds. For instance, the systemic significance of fraud, success, contraction, succession and licenses.

Field of Connection

Jan Jacob Stam
What is a good place for me? How come I keep taking the responsibility for something that isn't mine? How do we figure out the right direction for the change process again? Which job description fits the new manager best? Which position can I take as director of an organisation that services social services for youth? How will the market respond to this new product? In this book, Jan Jacob answers the questions of participants in hia workshops with constellations. He takes you through the process in a few constellations so you can experience the power they have.

Follow Jan Jacob and Barbara in their blogs here:
`www.hellingerinstituut.com` and
sign up for the newsletter to keep yourself informed and nurtured.

Sources and Literature

To be able to write this book, we have drawn upon more sources than we can mention here.

Our most important source are the participants in our workshops and seminars and all those companies and organisations all over the world, that invited us over the past 18 years to work together with them on issues they were dealing with. We feel deep gratitude for having been called into organisations and into, sometimes delicate, situations. We are grateful for the trust people have put in us, despite their scepticism and suspicions. But mainly we are grateful for all the insights we took from these hundreds of situations, Insights that will hopefully be to the advantage of others.

A second important source are our colleagues from the Bert Hellinger Institute in The Netherlands and all colleagues in and outside of Holland with whom we exchanged endlessly, tested new insights with, rejected them, until they were ripe enough to bring the insights and wisdom in our work.

Literature is a third, more limited source for us. We tend to figure out more than read. We have listed the list of literature sources to the most important books and the sources mentioned in the chapters. As a directive for interested readers: please go online for the most up-to-date insights and editions.

Bert Hellinger

Our most important source and teacher in the field of systemic phenomenological work. 'The art of Helping', 'Success in work and life', 'Bewegingen van de Geest' are just a few of the books he wrote who can be referred to, to deepen your knowledge. More importantly, Hellinger is himself still, always. Searching new insights.

Anton de Kroon

Systemic Consulting. A practical book for consultants and anyone who wants to change, improve, understand how his or her team works.

CHAPTER 6. TRANSFORMATION

Heather Plett

Heather Plett writes blogs on Holding Space. About 'how to hold space for others' as well as 'How to hold space for yourself'. And 'holding liminal space'. You can sing up on her website to receive her blogs: www.heatherpratt.com

Otto Scharmer

MIT Boston, USA developed Theory U, a process about significant changes in organisations and society. The book 'Theory U', was published in 2011 in the Netherlands. On the website of the Presencing Institute you can find many summaries and new developments in this field of work. www.presencing.com

Daniel Siegel

Mindsight is about how, through focused attention of our minds, we can activate thoughts, feelings and underdeveloped parts of our mind and how integration in our nervous system and be achieved. This method is very complementary to systemic work and constellations.

Bibi Schreuder

Bibi Schreuder is an important source. Bibi's focus is always on the foundation. The building blocks of the systemic work have to check out. In an unstoppable flow of professionalism, Bibi will sharpen these building blocks until they are exactly right in form, texture and firmness. And in a way that the blocks fit the bigger picture.

Jan Jacob Stam

Jan Jacob Stam (1954) studied Biology and later Didactics. *"Through the study of Biology, I increasingly started loving living systems. Of course, it is also where I learned to think analytically, but it also sowed the seeds for the way I perceive phenomenologically. I once promised myself to understand more about what patterns really are, and now I am starting to deliver on that promise."*

Jan Jacob worked in more 'difficult' forms of education for ten years. *"Through teaching, I started to love how people learn and develop. Now, years later, I find I am only just starting to understand it a little. I enjoy new insights the most. I am happiest, when I come into situations where I can learn new insights. Knowledge wants to flow. I enjoy developing as well as making knowledge available in a setting of co-creation."*

Jan Jacob worked for the Dutch (State) telecommunication Company, PTT-telecom for a few years, after which he continued as management consultant and partner in a consultancy for 10 years. *"The most important thing I learned during those years, is to wish people and organisations their own troubles. I am not a helper by nature, and it works out. I acknowledge that the work that I do, can have a great supporting effect. But helping is not what deeply drives me."*

In 1995, Jan Jacob came into contact with constellations, experienced many, went to many seminars of Bert Hellinger and other pioneers in the field. In 2000 Jan Jacob and his wife Bibi Schreuder founded the Bert Hellinger Institute the Netherlands. He works in well over thirty countries, wrote five books, organised Dutch and International congresses. He is the absolute forerunner in development of systemic work in organisations. He introduced many new terms and concepts, 'systemic' being one of them. *"And the end of the development of systemic work is still a long way away."*

Barbara Hoogenboom

Barbara Hoogenboom (1972) studied business administration at the University of Nyenrode, and graduated with a Bachelor's degree; at the University of Oregon (U.S.A.) she graduated with a Bachelor's in Management and Marketing.

> *"Practical application, highly professional and a broad, International orientation, were the components that appealed to me in these studies. How special to realise that these components still appeal to me, to this day, in my work at the Bert Hellinger Institute Netherlands."*

Barbara worked for more than a decade for an international bank and insurer in Holland as well as on the Dutch Antilles and Aruba. Mostly in commercially oriented middle management functions. After that, she worked as a mediator for ten years and was the forerunner in a divorce-specific mediation concept, which she founded in The Netherlands. She has mediated in many conflicts in small, medium sized and large organisations in the profit and not-for profit sector.

> *"As mediator, I quickly learned that a problem or conflict 'wasn't mine'. I did, however, feel responsible to help the people involved to new insights and solutions in a professional way, with a non-judgmental attitude."*

In 2012, she did the 'System Dynamics in Organisations' course at the Bert Hellinger Institute the Netherlands (BHIN), after which she followed many more at BHIN. She also participated in many international seminars in Holland and outside of the country, with Bert and Sophie Hellinger, Stephan Hausner, Christine Blumenstein, Judith Hemming, Arawana Hayashi, Matthias Varga von Kibed and Insa Sparrer and many more.

In 2014, she became trainer at BHIN and in 2015, Barbara became co-owner with Jan Jacob Stam and Bibi Schreuder. Since that time, she has dedicated her time fully to bringing systemic phenomenological work further into the world.

"I feel like a door, a portal. A gateway to logical language and practical use and all the enriching insights that go with this work. Somewhere, deeply, people know this. It is just that language and form is missing. Once you go through the portal, it will be within your reach."

CHAPTER 6. TRANSFORMATION

Guest writers

(L.B.) Lucel Bont

Lucel Bont leads the team Recovery of the municipality's tax office for five municipalities in the province of Groningen, the Netherlands. He has done many courses at the Bert Hellinger Institute. Amongst others, he followed the course the System Dynamics in Organisations. In combination with his communication background, Lucel benefits from his systemic perspective in his work and as front man in the preparations for a Northern Tax Office. lucelbont@gmail.com

(I.O.) Ietze Oostinga

Ietze Oostinga works as program manager and (project) coach at the municipality of Apeldoorn and as an independent consultant and coach. Connecting people is his passion. On the inside (head, heart, pelvis) as well as people with each other. This is why he coaches 1-on-1, gives workshops and guides organisational development. When the connections are strained or blocked, he uses his systemic skills.

To improve his mastery of systemic work, he graduated form a three year programme at ITIP (internal connection), a course in 'deep (systemic) coaching' at the Alba Academy (1-on-1 connection) and the course System Dynamics in organisations at the Hellinger Institute (1-ro-more connection). iwoostinga@gmail.com

(W.P.) Willem Plomp

"I work for a foundation for primary education in Amsterdam, 20 elementary schools, 6000 children, 600 staff members. I fulfilled many a role there: educator, coach, project leader, manager. I acted on many different layers: the board of directors, managers and teachers, of educational institutes and of schools. I experienced the different organisational models, varying from orderly hierarchically structured small units to more complex partnerships of larger institutions. In Amsterdam, where everything is always in transition, where new land is made, where old land gets new destinations, where groups of people move, where infinity and new beginnings go hand in hand."

(A.R.) Abelius Reitsma

Abelius Reitsma works at the Hanze University of Applied Sciences in Groningen. At the staff agency of Education and Research, he manages thirty professionals divided in a few consultancy teams. Abeluis followed many courses on systemic work when he worked as a consultant at Hanze. With his systemic weight, the step into a management position was a logical step. `a.reitsma@pl.hanze.nl`

(M.L.) Marion Latour

Over the past 19 years, Marion has worked in various tactical and strategic management positions at the Fire Department and the Police Force, where she now works as a manager. IN 2013, she came into contact with systemic work and since then she has combined the systemic wisdom & knowledge in leading organisations.

> *"For me, systemic leadership is being able to stand at the very edge of the systems, you can step in and out of them to take and use the information you find."*

Bert Hellinger Institute the Netherlands

The Bert Hellinger Institute the Netherlands (BHIN) was founded by Jan Jacob Stam and Bibi Schreuder in 2000 and since 2015, Barbara Hoogenboom is co-owner.

Bert Hellinger encouraged Jan Jacob to take this step and allowed him to use his name. To this day, we are in regular contact and exchange with Bert Hellinger, now 91 years old.

What characterizes BHIN is:

- On the one hand, the loyalty to the foundation of the systemic phenomenological work the way Bert Hellinger discovered and described it. Working with the consciences, the principles (workings) and the patterns that arise;

- On the other hand, the continuing, phenomenological, openness to what wants to develop and reveal itself. This means for example, that we look at this work and the role of facilitator in constellations in a different way than in 2000. And that we have said our farewell to habits and interventions that were previously customary.

We can imagine, and even encourage the participants in our courses, to incorporate systemic work in their 'own toolkit' with their other 'tools'. That they develop their own style and mix. But with the implicit assumption that people are clear in their communication about their mixture.

This is only possible, if at BHIN we stay, as purely and precisely as possible, close to the foundations or the phenomenological work. That is what we enjoy most, and with a lot of love. Ánd that is what we want people to recognise us for, both meanings of the word, in the outside world.

More information and contact:
info@hellingerinstituut.nl
www.hellingerinstituut.nl

About Barbara Piper

Barbara Piper (1972) grew up in a fully bi-lingual household with an English father and a Dutch mother. After an international education in both The Netherlands and abroad, she finished the International Baccalaureate and graduated from the University of Groningen, The Netherlands, with a Master's degree in Communication and English.

Barbara's professional career has been in business as well as in health care. After more than a decade in communication positions in corporate environments, she changed to the role of managing director in Health Care institutes. She gained a solid position as organisational advisor in the Netherlands with systemic work at the core of her approach and her own education for more than 10 years.

Today, she lives with her family in San Francisco. Barbara works as a life coach and facilitator of Lifeshops. She supports people as they deal with issues like change and decision-making, both career oriented or personal issues. At the heart of her work lies inner-work and reflection. Barbara is a written and oral poet and is on her way to publishing her first manuscript.

For Systemic Coaching, Barbara has a double-hatted position. As translator and as publisher. Together with Siets Bakker, she founded Systemic Books, an International Digital Publishing House. Their purpose is to contribute to the development, publication and advancement of Systemic works worldwide through digital publications.

About Systemic Books

Systemic Books is an international independent Publishing House focused on creating high quality content selected from the broad range of books available. The books range from classic to cutting edge work with new adaptations of the systemic school of thought and working. This way, Systemic Books aims to answer to the different levels of knowledge people have or need on systemic work.

Systemic Books wass founded in joint energy by Siets Bakker and Barbara Piper in 2016. When they met in 2015, their knowledge of and interest in the systemic perspective and their shared love for books, planted the seed for Systemic Books. This initiative combines their knowledge in the publishing world and efforts to make systemic work available to a global audience. We translate, edit and publish books. Great books about the systemic school of thought. We make use of all modern possibilities in publishing and printing to make these books available all over the world.

More information and contact:
contact@systemicbooks.com
www.systemicbooks.com

Index

acknowledging, 1, 6, 12, **17**, 19, 20, 22, 51, 58, 62, 75, 78, 89, 92, 94, 100, 103, 104, 108, 110, 119, 131, 138, 153, 157, 175, 179, 186, 189, 200, 203, 213, 225
agency, 50, **69**, 70, 71, 98, 188, 212
Anton de Kroon, *see* Kroon
autonomy, 6, 50, **68**, 70, 98, 109, 123, 137, 158

ba, **207**, 211
belonging, 34, 38, 42, 46, 72, **78**, 92, 103, 198, 202
Bert Hellinger, *see* Hellinger

change, 6, 17, 20, 47, 76, 84, 91, **154**, 166, 169, 194, 196, 204
communio, 69, 98
completeness, 42, 43, 56, **78**, 96
conflict of loyalty, *see* loyalty
conscience, *see* unit conscience, system conscience
constellation, **8**, 9, 18, 33, 58, 71, 76, 79, 81, 84, 101, 123, 145, 147, 150, 165, 185, 209, 216, 221
contribution, 15, 43, 47, 51, 80, 90, 94, **103**, 128, 129, 177, 191

destination, 6, 34, 40, 43, 54, **58**, 77, 106, 129, 144, 182, 184
disrupting, 39, 62, 65, 96, 101, 115, 119, **123**, 126, 191, 204
double binds, 160, **166**, 167–169

emerging future, **60**, 61, 78, 83, 181, 197, 201, 204, 206, 208, 210, 220
emerging past, **62**, 64
evolutionary force, **39**, 40, 41, 58, 60, 72, **77**, 123, 181, 182, 195, 197, **204**, 206

exchange, 22, 34, 43, 47, **53**, 55, 57, 93, 103, 106, 111, 175, 201
exclusion, 37, **56**, 152, 156

family business, 81, **88**
father's daughters, **128**
finiteness, 34, 43, **58**
flow, 1, 30, 56, 65, 69, 71, 73, 104, 107, **108**, 120
founder, 79, 83, 104, 145, 171, 207
function, 14, 40, 42, 43, 47, **50**, 52, 57, 70, 82, **86**, 87–90, 93, 96, 98, 102, 111, 130, 155, **174**, 185, 187, 197
funding, **108**, 111

growing beyond, **122**, 163, 165

habit, 29, 36, **114**
healing movement, 17, **18**
Hellinger, Bert, 20, 32, 59, 60, 84, 104, 206, 208, 223, 225, 230

identification, **152**, 154–157, 171

Kroon, Anton de, 21, 224

leadership, *see* systemic leadership
leading principle, 6, **47**, 50, 57, 73, 77, **94**, 99, 111, 179, 202
leading principle, 97, 186
life energy, 65, 97, **108**, 182, 185, 213

liminal space, 209, 212
loyalty, 22, 44, 64, 76, 84, 88, **91**, 154, 156, 182

middle management, 71, 94, **99**, 138, 226
money, 22, 54, 63, 81, 84, 97, 98, 108, 109, **110**, 140, 161, 170, 218
mother's sons, **127**, 129, 188

not-knowing, **30**, 204

order, 6, 34, 42, **46**, 47, 49, 51, **57**, 73, 77, 86, 90, **93**, 96, **98**, 101, 112, 115, 123, 126, 166, 182, 187, **202**
order of interventions, **214**
origin, 65, **79**, 80, 82, 118, 122, 207, 210
ownership, *see* systemic ownership

parentification, 96, 101, **132**, 134, 136–138, 180
patterns, 1, 6, 8, 12, 15, 16, 25, 39, 40, 57, 64, 73, 76, 79, 110, **114**, 116, 117, 119, 120, 122–124, 128, 129, 136, 169, 174, 181, 182, 188, 202–204, 214, 225
perception, *see* systemic perception
phenomenological, 23, 26, 32, 151, 223
place, 6, 25, 34, 42, 43, 46, 54, 57, 73, 78, **85**, 87, 88,

90, 91, **93**, 96, 98, 111, 114, 127, 133, 158, 170, 178, 187, 201, 206, 221
polarities, 158, **160**, 163, 165
position, 1, 16, 50, 57, 64, 72, 98, 101, 107, 111, 114, 116, 123, 128, 131, 133, 134, 136, 138, 139, 141, 150, 169, 179, 199, 202, 205, 209
presence, **176**
present, **104**, 140, 163, 164, 206, 208, 211
procedure, 32, **114**

rebel, 6, 76, 94, **102**, 104, 137, 174

seniority, 46, 47, 52, 94, **105**
survival mechanisms, 12, **33**, 42, 72, 78, 114, 196, 200
system-conscience, **37**, 39, 57, 82, 127, 135, 152, 171, 182, **202**, 206
systemic, **12**
systemic leadership, 1, 20, 47, 54, **68**, 76, 77, 79, 81, 88, 96, 108, 194, 229
systemic ownership, **83**, 109, 194, 206
systemic perception, 26, 27, 30
systems, 12, **15**, 148, 183

the whole, *see* whole
transformation, 7, 39, 59, 64, 74, 78, **194**, 195–197, 199, 201–204, 206, 211, 213, **214**, 218
transition, 77, 156, **194**, 196, 229
triangulation, 120, **125**, 126, 127, 130–132

unit-conscience, **35**, 37, 39, 57, 182, 206, 215, 216
untangling, 119, **120**, 138

whole, the, 1, 13, 23, **27**, 29, 32, 50, 70, 73, 85, 90, 94, 98, **103**, 106, 131, 190, 191, 217, 220

ya, **208**, 209, 211

Made in the USA
Las Vegas, NV
05 July 2024